Early Childhood Theorists and Approaches Explained

Chloe Webster

LONDON AND NEW YORK

Designed cover image: © Getty Images

First published 2025
by Routledge
4 Park Square, Milton Park, Abingdon, Oxon OX14 4RN

and by Routledge
605 Third Avenue, New York, NY 10158

Routledge is an imprint of the Taylor & Francis Group, an informa business

© 2025 Chloe Webster

The right of Chloe Webster to be identified as author of this work has been asserted in accordance with sections 77 and 78 of the Copyright, Designs and Patents Act 1988.

All rights reserved. No part of this book may be reprinted or reproduced or utilised in any form or by any electronic, mechanical, or other means, now known or hereafter invented, including photocopying and recording, or in any information storage or retrieval system, without permission in writing from the publishers.

Trademark notice: Product or corporate names may be trademarks or registered trademarks, and are used only for identification and explanation without intent to infringe.

British Library Cataloguing-in-Publication Data
A catalogue record for this book is available from the British Library

ISBN: 978-1-032-69135-0 (hbk)
ISBN: 978-1-032-69133-6 (pbk)
ISBN: 978-1-032-69136-7 (ebk)

DOI: 10.4324/9781032691367

Typeset in Optima
by Apex CoVantage, LLC

Early Childhood Theorists and Approaches Explained

This new book provides accessible explanations of the key theories, concepts, and approaches that form the foundations of early childhood education. Unpicking terms like "attachment," "constructivism," and "heuristic play" and introducing both established and less-known contemporary theorists, it is designed to be an easy and comprehensive guide to early childhood theories and approaches, an often complex topic to understand and explore fully.

The book is divided into two parts. The first provides a brief overview of the theorists and approaches, both historical and modern, with explanations, backgrounds, benefits, and criticisms where appropriate. It also defines key terms used in theory and research alongside examples of how they work in practice. Part 2 looks more broadly at how these theories and approaches have been incorporated into settings and present-day policies. The chapters also offer insights from practitioners on how the theories are used successfully and how different countries and cultures adopt and implement particular approaches.

This latest book in the *Key Concepts in Early Childhood Series* is essential reading for early years practitioners and students who want to support their studies and deepen their understanding, as it makes the pedagogical theories behind the early years curriculum and framework easy to understand and apply.

Chloe Webster is a former practitioner and childminder with a wealth of experience in the sector.

Key Concepts of Early Childhood

Series Editor: Tamsin Grimmer

This exciting new series unpicks key terms and concepts in early childhood education and shows how they relate to everyday practice. Each book focuses on a core theme and provides clear, concise definitions of key terminology alongside case studies and then explores how these link to core areas of provision.

Wellbeing Explained
Sonia Mainstone-Cotton

Loving Pedagogy Explained
Tamsin Grimmer

Early Childhood Theorists and Approaches Explained
Chloe Webster

For more information about this series, please visit: Key Concepts in Early Childhood—Book Series—Routledge & CRC Press

Contents

Acknowledgements	viii
A note from the editor	ix
Introduction	1
Part 1 Explaining terms	**5**
Ainsworth (Strange Situation)—see Attachment theory	7
Anti-racist practice	8
Athey (assimilation, accommodation)—see Schema theory	10
Attachment theory	13
Bandura	14
Bavolek	16
Beach schools	18
Belsky	21
Bourdieu	22
Bowlby (see Attachment theory)	23
Bronfenbrenner	24
Bruner	26
Chomsky	28
Curiosity Approach	30
Dewey	31
Dweck	32
Erikson	34
Forest schools	37
Freire	39

CONTENTS

Freud	41
Froebel	42
Gussin-Paley	46
Goldschmidt (see also Heuristic play and treasure baskets)	47
Helicopter Stories	48
Heuristic Play and Treasure Baskets	52
High/Scope	54
Hygge	56
In-The-Moment Planning	59
Isaacs	63
Key Person Approach (see Attachment theory)	65
Kohlberg	66
Laevers	69
Loving Pedagogy	71
Malaguzzi (see Reggio Emelia)	73
Maslow	74
McMillan	75
Montessori	77
Parten	79
Pavlov	81
Pedagogy	83
Piaget (see also Schema theory)	84
Pikler approach	86
Professional Love	88
Reggio Emelia	90
Scaffolding (see Bruner and Vygotsky): Schema theory	93
Skinner	95
Slow Pedagogy	97
Steiner	98
Te Whāriki	100
Trauma-Informed Practice or Trauma-Responsive Practice	102
Treasure Baskets (see also Heuristic play)	104
Vygotsky	105

Waldorf (see Steiner: Winnicott)	106
Zone of Proximal Development (see also Vygotsky)	108
Conclusion of Part 1	109
Further Reading and Resources	110
References	123
Part 2 Applying these theories to practice	**131**
The importance of embedding theories/approaches that encapsulate the beliefs of the setting as a community	133
How settings can begin to incorporate and follow new beliefs/ideas/approaches	134
Staff training	135
Parental involvement	136
Challenges of embedding new theories and approaches	137
Benefits of adopting/embedding new theories and approaches to early childhood education	138
Behavioural implications of adopting new theories and approaches	139
How to write a policy on pedagogy	141
Questions for reflection	144
Conclusion	145
References	146
Index	147

Acknowledgements

A huge thank-you to the following people and settings, whom this book wouldn't have been possible without. Thank you so much for your time, insights, and contributions.

In alphabetical order, a huge thank you to:

Camilla Lelliot-Berry
Cinnamon Brow CE Primary School Nursery
Elizabeth Luckhurst
Guildford Nursery School
Jack and Jill Preschool
Kate Bate
Little Rascals Day Nursery
Marlis Juerging-Coles
Nicky Gare-Mogg
Sally Cave
Sharon Ashworth-Leach
Tamsin Grimmer

A note from the editor

This book is part of a new series from Routledge, which I am thrilled to be editing. I first got the idea for this series when talking with several practitioners about the definitions of terms I used in my own work around loving pedagogy. I realised it would be helpful to have an amplified dictionary unpicking the terms used and explaining what they mean and look like in practice. Then I thought, if this idea would work well for explaining a loving pedagogy, it might also work well for other topics, and the idea of Key Concepts in Early Childhood was formed.

This particular book, *Early Childhood Theories and Approaches Explained*, written by Chloe, is the third in the series, and the idea arose from my work with practitioners in training including undergraduates and post-graduate teacher training. I noticed that many students and practitioners do a web search for a topic or phrase before researching thoroughly to give them an overview of a theme. Sometimes, the results of these searches were not reliable or credible and would be unhelpful in the field of early childhood. Therefore, I envisioned a book which could act like a one-stop shop, outlining briefly some of the key theories and approaches we come across but within an early childhood lens, and the idea of *Early Childhood Theories and Approaches Explained* was born!

Chloe begins by considering the rationale for using theory and exploring different approaches in practice, and she then unpicks specific terms used in relation to theories and approaches, including some key named theorists and pedagogical approaches. At the end of the first section, Chloe shares lots of helpful resources and suggestions for further reading. Then, in Part 2, she explores how settings can incorporate theory and different approaches into practice, considering areas such

A NOTE FROM THE EDITOR

as staff training, parental involvement, challenges that may be encountered, and how to write a policy in more detail.

It was a joy to edit this book, and I know you will learn from Chloe's clear explanations and enjoy dipping into the different sections. I hope this book assists you in learning about the theories and approaches that have influenced early childhood as we know it today.

Tamsin Grimmer, Series Editor

Introduction

The early years curriculum encompasses and is the result of years of research, experiments, theories, investigations, and critical reflections from a diverse range of professionals and experts in neuroscience, child development, psychology, and education. In addition, settings may choose to adopt a specific pedagogical approach which underpins their practice. Theories and approaches within early childhood education help us to understand how children develop and learn. Each theory or approach provides an insight or different perspective from which to view the child and work in practice. They are all valid in their own way, and sometimes, early childhood practitioners find it difficult to decide where to start when looking into them.

By basing our practice on evidence-informed practices and keeping up to date with theories, approaches, and research and how these change, develop, and can be applied to modern-day practice, we are not only deepening our understanding of early childhood education and child development, thus making us better practitioners, but we are also providing the best possible experiences and learning opportunities for children

This book provides an overview of the most important and influential early childhood theorists and pedagogies to better support your understanding of early childhood development, the theories and approaches it is based upon, and how our curriculum and pedagogies have changed over time.

Rationale for *Early Childhood Theorists and Approaches Explained*

This book is designed to be an easy comprehensive guide to early childhood theories and approaches, an often complex topic to unpick and explore fully, but the aim of this book is to make complex historical concepts and ideas accessible to anyone in the early years sector, regardless of their qualification level, to support their practice and cement their knowledge of theory to enable them to put it into practice.

I hope that this book will also be a supportive and accessible learning resource for students gaining their qualifications in early childhood, a handy, easy-to-read source of information to support their studies and deepen their understanding of the key theories and approaches to early education.

Layout of book

Part 1 of this book is designed to unpick the many different early years theorists and approaches that you will encounter as an educator in the early years sector. It can be dipped into, as the terms are ordered alphabetically, and topics can also be found from the contents page and the index. Each term is fully but succinctly explained, and some terms also have examples from practice which further exemplify them.

In between Parts 1 and 2 is a Further Reading and Resources section, which is designed to support you as the reader and signpost you to additional information and resources.

Part 2 will look more broadly at the ethos of the setting/school and unpick several aspects of *Early Childhood Theorists and Approaches Explained*, including:

- The importance of embedding theories/approaches that encapsulate the beliefs of the setting as a community
- How settings can begin to incorporate and follow new beliefs/ideas/approaches
- Staff training
- Parental involvement

- Challenges they may face in doing so
- Benefits of adopting/embedding new theories and approaches to early childhood education
- How to write a policy on pedagogy
- Behavioural implications of adopting new theories and approaches

At the end of the book, you can find any references referred to in Parts 1 and 2. They are linked to the text throughout the book using superscript numbers. I am using the term "setting" very broadly in this book to encompass childminders, schools, and private, voluntary, and independent settings. In a similar vein, the term "practitioner" includes all adults who work alongside children regardless of their level of qualification or experience. I am using the term "parents" to include not only birth parents but also any main carers of a child, for example, grandparents, foster carers, or step-parents. Children are referred to using pseudonyms, and wherever possible, children have also been consulted about the use of any case study material or photographs. I have also tried to consider representation of backgrounds, cultural heritage, settings, and gender to try and ensure this book shares the perspective of others.

Who am I?

Before we start the book, I thought it appropriate to introduce myself fully! I have more than 15 years' experience in the early years sector and have worked in a number of roles, from private day nurseries to after-school clubs, as well as becoming a childminder and a nanny. I have also been a senior room leader, playworker, and qualified early years SENCo. I am also an early years author who has been published in several early years magazines, books, and journals across the sector.

I live in West Sussex with my husband and young daughter and love walks by the sea, yoga, and reading.

Part 1 | Explaining terms

In this section I will be exploring key terms relating to early childhood theories and approaches. It is designed to be dipped into and out of as readers explore these words and phrases. The following terms will be explored:

Ainsworth
Anti-racist practice
Athey
Attachment theory
Bandura
Bavolek
Beach schools
Belsky
Bourdieu
Bowlby
Bronfenbrenner
Bruner
Chomsky
Curiosity Approach
Dewey
Dweck
Erikson
Forest schools
Freire
Freud
Froebel
Goldschmidt

Gussin-Paley
Helicopter Stories
Heuristic Play and Treasure Baskets
High/Scope
Hygge
In-The-Moment Planning
Issacs
Key Person Approach
Kohlberg
Laevers
Loving Pedagogy
Malaguzzi
Maslow
McMillan
Montessori
Parten
Pavlov
Pedagogy
Piaget
Pikler approach
Professional Love
Reggio Emelia

Scaffolding
Schema theory
Skinner
Slow Pedagogy
Steiner
Te Whāriki

Trauma-Informed Practice
Treasure baskets
Vygotsky
Waldorf
Winnicott
Zone of Proximal Development

Ainsworth (Strange Situation)—see Attachment theory

Mary Ainsworth[1] was a prominent developmental psychologist renowned for her groundbreaking work on attachment theory. Building on Bowlby's attachment theory, Ainsworth's contribution was the development of the "Strange Situation" procedure and the identification of attachment styles. Conducted in the late 1960s, Ainsworth's study revolutionised our comprehension of how infants bond with their caregivers and navigate the world around them. The insights of these studies continue to reverberate through the field of early childhood education, shaping approaches and interventions aimed at fostering secure attachments and healthy emotional development in young children today.

The Strange Situation involved a controlled observational study designed to assess the quality of an infant's attachment to their caregiver. Through a series of structured separations and reunions, Ainsworth identified three primary attachment patterns: secure, insecure-avoidant, and insecure-resistant.[2] (Main and Solomon[3] later expanded this to include a fourth pattern; disorganised).

Ainsworth's research has been instrumental in understanding the critical role of early relationships in shaping a child's emotional and social development. The findings of her work underscore the significance of responsive caregiving and the establishment of secure attachment relationships between practitioners and young learners. Practitioners play a pivotal role in providing a supportive framework wherein children feel valued, understood, and emotionally secure. By fostering secure attachments, practitioners lay the foundation for children's emotional resilience, social competence, and overall well-being.

Anti-racist practice

Anti-racist practice in the early years refers to the positive impact practitioners can have on their overall practice and pedagogy by developing their own knowledge and understanding of systematic racism, by critically reflecting on their provision and through ensuring that they embed an anti-racist and inclusive approach in every aspect of their provision.

Anti-racism in early childhood education entails actively challenging and dismantling systems of oppression, prejudice, and discrimination based on race. It involves fostering an environment in which every child feels valued, respected, and represented regardless of their racial or ethnic background. It goes beyond mere acceptance to celebrate diversity and promote equality.[4]

Creating an inclusive learning environment begins with the physical space. Settings and classrooms should reflect the diversity of the children they serve, with materials, books, toys, and images representing various races, cultures, and ethnicities. Incorporating multicultural perspectives into the curriculum helps children develop empathy, understanding, and appreciation for different backgrounds.

Identity development starts early, and practitioners play a pivotal role in shaping how children perceive themselves and others. Anti-racist practices involve affirming and validating children's racial and cultural identities while challenging stereotypes and biases. Through literature, discussions, and activities, practitioners can promote positive self-esteem and pride in one's heritage.

Implicit bias is a negative attitude, one of which we are not consciously aware, against a specific social group. Implicit biases often seep into interactions, even in early childhood settings. Educators must be vigilant in recognising and addressing their own biases while actively countering stereotypes that may arise among children. Open discussions about race and diversity, facilitated with age-appropriate language, help dispel misconceptions and promote critical thinking.[5]

Athey (assimilation, accommodation)—see Schema theory

Chris Athey writes about schemas and schematic play which highlight the importance of active learning and holistic development in early childhood. She uses the terms "assimilation" and "accommodation" to talk about how children's ideas about the world grow and develop. Athey built on the work of Piaget, which looks at how children construct understanding through firsthand experience.

Athey defines a "schema" as "a pattern of repeatable behaviour into which experiences are assimilated and that are gradually co-ordinated. Co-ordinations lead to higher- level and more powerful schemas."[6]

"Assimilation" refers to the process through which individuals incorporate new information or experiences into their existing cognitive structures or, put another way, how children's brains accept new learning. Co-ordinated in this context means that the child's thinking is accepted into their understanding about a concept. In the context of early childhood education, assimilation involves children actively engaging with their environment, exploring, experimenting, and making sense of the world around them through play and hands-on experiences and learning through this.

Accommodation refers to when a child is actively engaging with their environment but their play challenges what they already know about the world, so they have to accommodate their thinking in the light of their new experiences. For example, if a child is rolling balls and then tries to roll a rugby ball, the ball would not roll in the same way as a round ball. The child would need to accommodate or change their thinking to allow for this new information.

Athey's work on schemas has been pivotal in supporting adults in understanding the importance of repetition in children's play and

DOI: 10.4324/9781032691367-5

subsequent learning. Implementing Athey's approach involves creating rich, stimulating environments that encourage exploration, creativity, and critical thinking.

SCHEMAS IN PRACTICE

When creating and setting up an early years environment it is essential to think about schematic play in terms of the physical space and what is on offer and how these provide opportunities for children to explore schemas in their child-led play. This is why, as practitioners, we should be providing open-ended materials and resources for children to explore, manipulate, and use as they wish rather than with a pre-determined purpose or outcome in mind.

When thinking about schemas and how we can provide an environment that promotes schematic opportunities we should be thinking about providing materials and resources like:

- Cotton reels
- Balls
- Scarves
- Boxes
- Pine cones or other natural objects
- Bags and/or baskets

However, we should also consider the physical space available and if it is set up in a way that children feel they have ownership and opportunity to use the space how they need to. For example, are all the shelves/windowsills/tops of units already full of toys and resources? Can children line up objects on top of surfaces? Children need space to explore and arrange their play, and so we should ensure we don't overfill or clutter our learning environments to enable them to do so.

Similarly, are their spaces for them to climb into boxes or hide between units and tables if this is where there play takes them? Is there somewhere they can drop/roll balls?

These are all important things we need to consider when thinking about schemas and how they fit into our physical environments and room plans.

Attachment theory

Attachment theory is one of the most well-known theories in early childhood education and refers to a child's emotional bond with another person. Attachment theory was a concept first coined by John Bowlby,[7] a British psychiatrist. Bowlby believed that the early bonds formed by children to their caregivers have an impact that stays with them for a lifetime—making these early attachments the most important of a child's life. Bowlby also believed that these early attachments kept the baby close to their mother, subsequently increasing their chances of survival.[8]

Mary Ainsworth[1] was another pivotal figure in the field of developmental psychology and, along with Bowlby, was renowned for her groundbreaking work on attachment theory. Ainsworth, an American-Canadian developmental psychologist, expanded upon Bowlby's original work through her "Strange Situation" experiment. This study identified different attachment styles in children: secure, anxious-avoidant, and anxious-ambivalent. These classifications highlighted how early relationships shape a child's capacity for trust, self-regulation, and exploration.

In early childhood education, understanding attachment theory is fundamental. Armed with this knowledge, practitioners can create environments that support secure attachments, fostering a sense of safety and trust for young children. By recognising and nurturing these early bonds, practitioners play a crucial role in promoting healthy emotional development and laying the groundwork for future relationships. Attachment theory is present and "in action" in settings worldwide through the "key person approach" that all settings are required to implement in some way to support the emotional well-being of all children (see Key person).

Bandura

Albert Bandura[9] proposed the "social learning theory," which later developed into "social cognitive theory." It suggests that children learn through observing, imitating, and modelling others' behaviour. This theory explains that children acquire new behaviours and knowledge by watching others, a process known as vicarious learning. Children learn by observing and imitating the behaviour of others, particularly influential role models, but also through direct experience. Bandura argues that through the process of modelling, children acquire new skills, values, and attitudes, shaping their behaviour and cognitive processes.

His research stems from the famous and controversial "Bobo doll experiments," which subjected preschool-aged children to videos of adults responding, sometimes violently, to a doll. These experiments demonstrated that children learn through observing and imitating the behaviour of adults.

Bandura's social learning theory emerged as a counterpoint to the dominant behaviourist views of his time, which emphasised that all behaviours are learned through direct reinforcement or punishment.[10]

The key components of Bandura's social learning theory include:

- **Observational learning**—children learn by observing the behaviour of others.
- **Imitation and modelling**—Children tend to imitate behaviours modelled by individuals they consider authoritative or similar to themselves, such as parents, teachers, or peers.
- **Intrinsic reinforcement**—Unlike behaviourists, who emphasise external reinforcement, Bandura introduced the concept of intrinsic reinforcement, which includes internal rewards like pride,

satisfaction, and a sense of accomplishment, which can motivate children to replicate observed behaviours.
- **Reciprocal determinism**—Bandura highlighted that a child's environment, behaviour, and personal factors (such as cognition) interact in a dynamic and reciprocal manner. This means that while the environment influences the child, the child also influences the environment.[11]

Bandura's theories have had a profound impact on the field of early childhood education, providing practitioners with valuable insights into the power of modelling and the role of the social environment in children's learning and development.

CASE STUDY: IMITATION/ROLE-MODELLING—A NANNY PERSPECTIVE

I have looked after R since he was around 14 months old, and our routines have always been the same in terms of timing and how we navigate our day. Each time I would be preparing dinner, I would say out loud, "Almost dinner time. I will start cooking soon" and head into the kitchen to turn on the oven/boil the water to start the cooking process, often taking him into the kitchen with me to turn on the appliances.

Once R started moving and could move independently around the play space, each time I would announce I was about to start preparing dinner, he would crawl/walk over to the play kitchen and begin turning knobs, filling and arranging pans, and opening and closing the oven door. R is 2.5 years old now, and we still have this same routine, and he still accesses the play kitchen and imitates cooking and preparing food at the same time as I do.

Bavolek

Dr Stephen Bavolek is a renowned expert in early childhood education who has made significant contributions to the early years childhood education field with his influential theories. Bavolek emphasises the importance of nurturing a child's socio-emotional development, as it plays a crucial role in their overall well-being.

Bavolek's theory focuses on the concept of building resilience and promoting positive interactions within early childhood settings. He argues that by creating a supportive and caring environment, practitioners can empower children to develop essential skills such as self-control, empathy, and problem-solving abilities.

Bavolek's theory is built on several core principles:

1. **Nurturing relationships:** Central to Bavolek's theory is the belief that nurturing, supportive relationships between children and caregivers are essential for healthy development. These relationships provide a secure base from which children can explore the world and develop confidence and resilience.
2. **Empathy and understanding:** Bavolek emphasises the importance of empathy and understanding in interactions between adults and children. By recognising and responding to children's emotions and needs, caregivers can build trust and strengthen the parent–child bond.
3. **Positive discipline:** Rather than relying on punitive measures, Bavolek advocates for positive discipline techniques that focus on teaching and guiding children's behaviour. This approach helps children learn to regulate their emotions and develop self-control in a supportive environment.

4. **Resilience and coping skills:** Building resilience is a key component of Bavolek's theory. By providing children with opportunities to overcome challenges and develop coping skills, caregivers can help them navigate life's ups and downs more effectively.
5. **Community support:** Bavolek stresses the importance of community support systems in promoting child well-being. By creating networks of support for families, communities can enhance their capacity to provide nurturing environments for children.

Bavolek's theories have had a profound impact on the field of early childhood education, providing practitioners with valuable insights and strategies to promote healthy socio-emotional development in young learners. In addition to this, Bavolek promotes the importance of engagement between the parent and child as vital and highlights the benefits of the "nurturing care approach."[12]

Beach schools

Beach schools are a relatively new concept in early childhood education, emerging as a unique and innovative approach offering children the opportunity to learn and play in natural beach environments.

The idea originated from Scandinavia and with origins of beach school found within the forest school movement. "Williams-Siegfredsen states that the term Forest School describes the Danish practice where early years settings go outdoors, daily, to educate children."[13]

Beach schools focus on providing children with hands-on experiences in nature, allowing them to explore, discover, and connect with their surroundings. These outdoor classrooms offer a rich learning environment that stimulates sensory experiences, encourages physical activity, and fosters a deeper appreciation for the natural world.

By engaging in activities such as beachcombing, sandcastle building, and marine life observation, children develop important cognitive, social, and emotional skills. The development of beach schools highlights the growing recognition of the benefits of nature-based education and the importance of incorporating outdoor experiences into early childhood curriculums.

CASE STUDY: A NANNY'S PERSPECTIVE

During a beach school session, children are encouraged to explore the environment independently and all the changing landscapes, opportunities, and natural play experiences that the coastline offers, allowing these natural opportunities and natural play resources to shape their session as they explore, learn, and discover in their own way, in their own time, all the while gaining a deeper insight into their natural world.

Beach school sessions allow children the freedom, independence, and confidence to explore a vast array of natural play and learning experiences and facilitate and lead their own play and learning inspired by their natural world and the constantly changing environment as they gain a deeper insight into the natural world as they learn to observe tides and currents and gain a newfound respect for risk, water, and the elements. Experiential and in-the-moment learning constantly challenges the thought processes and curiosity of children alongside teaching them skills for life, and beach school sessions are a fantastic opportunity to support and develop this type of learning and these skills.

I am very lucky that my locality clearly means that a visit to the beach is an easy and frequent opportunity for us. In my opinion the innate curiosity in discovering elements of the natural world and children facilitating and meeting their own learning and development needs as they explore and investigate this natural play space is truly invaluable. There are, of course, safety elements to consider when using the beach as an additional outdoor classroom, particularly as this natural space is considerably unpredictable with the current and tide set to change your entire experience, but these variables are also invaluable learning opportunities for children of all ages.

Whilst the beauty of beach school is that planning is not required, and the over-arching principle is the children lead and facilitate their own learning based upon what they witness and experience throughout the session, it is important that an initial-boundary setting activity/experience is re-visited on numerous occasions whilst children adjust and become accustomed to the freedom, risk, and independence of these beach school sessions.

It is good practice to outline a parameter with the children within which they can independently explore and roam without adult support, and by setting these parameters, you are not only instilling boundaries for children but also promoting trust and independence, from which children will thrive and benefit significantly as a result.

My role in children's learning and development during these sessions is "the knowledgeable other," and I am a huge advocate of children being in charge of their own learning and development, and generally, I only step in to support when asked to by the children or in order to teach them a new skill or develop their learning in some way. Essentially, I am the facilitator of the environment, and my role is to support and develop the children's learning by introducing vocabulary and skills and to develop their understanding of the natural world, not to lead or change their play or interests for the sake of a pre-determined plan or agenda.

Outdoor play is not exclusive just for the summer months or more favourable weather, nor is beach school. Beach school should be offered to children throughout the year, regardless of the season or weather. The natural world itself changes with the seasons, and it is paramount that children are not only aware of these changes but experience and explore them firsthand

to cement their learning and bring learning full circle. No child is too young to be exposed to natural play and the elements, and the earlier we expose children to these experiences, the more confident and knowledgeable they will be within an outdoor environment as varied as the beach.

Belsky

Jay Belsky, a prominent researcher in the field of early childhood development, has made significant contributions to the understanding of how various factors influence children's development.

According to Belsky, his ecological model emphasises the complex interplay between biological, familial, and environmental factors in shaping a child's development. Belsky's theory highlights the importance of considering multiple influences, including genetic predispositions, parenting styles, and socio-economic conditions, in understanding children's outcomes.[14]

Belsky argues that a comprehensive understanding of early childhood development requires examining the dynamic interactions among these various factors. Belsky's theories have had a profound impact on informing policies and practices that aim to create supportive environments and promote optimal development for young children.[15]

Bourdieu

Pierre Bourdieu believes that "Cultural Capital" may play a role when individuals pursue power and status in society through politics or other means. Social and cultural capital along with economic capital contribute to the inequality we see in the world.[16]

According to Bourdieu and his theory, success in the education system is facilitated by the possession of cultural capital. However, education is not a way out of inequality but can negatively reinforce inequalities within society.[17] Cultural Capital is not something which can be taught, but it can perhaps be mitigated against.

In early years, Cultural Capital is interpreted slightly differently and refers to "the essential knowledge that pupils need to be educated citizens, introducing them to the best that has been thought and said and helping to engender an appreciation of human creativity and achievement" (Ofsted 2019).[18]

This socio-economic theory and approach has since been applied to early childhood education and children's possession of cultural capital within their early years. The value of this concept is now widely understood and identified by the sector as a key part of early childhood education and child development.[15] Practitioners are more aware of inequalities that may exist and try to build on their knowledge of children's backgrounds and experiences, attempting to address these inequalities.

Bowlby (see Attachment theory)

Attachment theory was a concept first coined by John Bowlby,[7] a British psychiatrist.

He emphasised the fundamental importance of early parent–child bonds for a child's emotional and social development. Bowlby believed that the early bonds formed by children to their caregivers have an impact that stays with them for a lifetime, making these early attachments the most important of a child's life. Bowlby also believed that these early attachments kept the baby close to their mother, subsequently increasing their chances of survival.

Bowlby's contributions to attachment theory highlight the importance of creating a nurturing and responsive learning environment. Educators are encouraged to build strong, supportive relationships with children, mirroring the security provided by a primary caregiver. This approach, which has been adopted in early years settings and schools across the country, helps children feel safe and valued, fostering their ability to explore, learn, and play.

When children develop secure attachments to their caregivers, they are significantly more likely to thrive emotionally, cognitively, and developmentally, because secure attachments build confidence and resilience and promote a child's overall emotional well-being, enabling them to access learning and play opportunities with confidence.

Bronfenbrenner

Urie Bronfenbrenner was a developmental psychologist whose "ecological systems theory" revolutionised the understanding of early childhood development by explaining that children do not grow in isolation; instead, they develop within a series of relationships.[19] His theory proposed that a child's development is influenced by a network of interconnected systems, each with its own unique characteristics and dynamics. These systems are depicted as concentric circles, with the child at the centre.

Bronfenbrenner's work emphasised the intricate interplay between a child's immediate environment and the broader social contexts that shape their growth. His theory was that a child's development is influenced by a series of nested systems,[20] including the following:

- Microsystem—direct interactions and influences from family and immediate surroundings, for example, a child's parents and carers, setting staff, nanny, childminder
- Exosystem—indirect influences on the child, for example, a parent's work pattern
- Macrosystem—larger cultural and societal influences on the child, for example, economic climate or cultural groups
- Mesosystem—interactions between the different systems, for example, how early childhood practitioners interact with parents or how parents interact with community groups
- Chronosystem—the impact that time has on all of these influences, for example, a child living through the COVID-19 pandemic will have a very different developmental pathway than a child growing up post-pandemic

This perspective emphasised the importance of considering the dynamic relationships between a child and their environment, acknowledging that development is not solely an individual process but rather a product of intricate interactions. Bronfenbrenner's groundbreaking approach has had a profound impact on the field of early childhood education and continues to guide practitioners, psychologists, and parents in fostering holistic and enriching environments for children today.[21]

Bruner

Jerome Bruner is a pioneering figure in the field of developmental psychology and made significant contributions to our understanding of early childhood education. Central to Bruner's approach is the concept of scaffolding, which he introduced as a framework for guiding a child's learning process.[22]

Drawing upon the metaphor of a scaffold in construction, Bruner emphasised the crucial role of more knowledgeable individuals, typically parents or practitioners, in providing structured support to a child as they navigate new concepts or tasks. This support is tailored to the child's current level of competence, gradually decreasing as the child gains mastery, as is the case when removing planks from a scaffold once a building becomes self-supporting.

Key principles of Bruner's scaffolding approach:

1. **Zone of Proximal Development (ZPD):** Central to Bruner's scaffolding concept is Vygotsky's idea of the zone of proximal development, which Bruner was influenced by.
2. **Structuring tasks:** Bruner advocated for breaking down complex tasks into manageable steps that align with a child's developmental stage. By presenting information in a structured and sequential manner, practitioners can scaffold children's learning effectively, ensuring gradual mastery of skills.
3. **Sensitive guidance:** Scaffolding requires practitioners to provide timely and sensitive guidance, adjusting their support based on children's progress and needs. This guidance can take various forms, such as modelling, questioning, prompting, or providing feedback, all aimed at helping children bridge the gap between what they know and what they are striving to learn.

4. **Gradual fading:** As children gain proficiency in a particular skill or concept, scaffolding should gradually diminish, allowing them to take on more responsibility for their learning. This process of fading ensures that children develop independence and self-regulation while still receiving support as needed.

Bruner also explained children's cognitive development and proposed a three-stage system or "modes of mental representation": enactive (when thinking is based on action and children learn through doing), iconic (when thinking is based on images or visual representation), and symbolic (when thinking can be more abstract and is based on language). Children's thought processes develop through these stages over time, and through adults' scaffolding their learning, children can understand difficult concepts. Early childhood practitioners would be using these ideas as they offer firsthand experiences to children and develop understanding by using visual aids or prompts and use language throughout the day.

He proposed that a concept is re-visited at a more sophisticated level as the child develops. Often referred to as the "spiral curriculum," this is when we may teach a child a concept, for example number or quantity, and build on this as we sing number songs, count more and more objects, and add more complex ideas to their developing mathematical understanding.

Bruner's theory highlights the importance of engaging children in meaningful, age-appropriate activities that stimulate their curiosity and problem-solving abilities, which ultimately foster a deeper, more enduring understanding of the "work" they do. His insights continue to shape early childhood education, highlighting the importance between adult guidance and a child's innate capacity for learning.

Chomsky

Noam Chomsky's[23] linguistic research in the 1950s aimed to understand the ways in which children acquire language. He proposed a system of principles and suggested that a child's understanding of syntax and semantics develop naturally.

Chomsky believed that rules for language acquisition are innate, meaning that all humans hold an inborn and natural capacity for language. Chomsky argues that language acquisition is not solely dependent on external factors but rather on the innate ability of the human brain to acquire grammatical categories and syntactic rules.[24]

At the heart of Chomsky's contributions is his theory of innate language acquisition. He proposed that children are born with an inherent ability to learn language, a concept known as "universal grammar." This theory suggests that the ability to acquire language is hardwired into the brain, enabling children to understand and produce language relatively quickly and effortlessly.

Noam Chomsky's approach to early childhood education is rooted in the belief that every child possesses innate potential that can be nurtured through a supportive, stimulating, and respectful learning environment. By emphasising natural language acquisition, critical thinking, creativity, and social awareness, practitioners can create a foundation for children to grow into thoughtful, independent, and engaged members of society.

CASE STUDY: A PRESCHOOL PERSPECTIVE

At our preschool, we understand that in order to effectively master language, we must give both opportunities to talk independently and provide play which fosters intrinsic motivation to talk in the first place.

This, paired with positive relationships in which children rest and feel loved and seen, stimulates, in our experience, language development that is relevant for each child and allows opportunities to broaden existent knowledge through open conversations.

One of our most valuable tools for early language development is our learning stories.

These comprise an account of a play situation experienced in close proximity to or alongside a child's key person. Such learning stories capture a special play moment and actual language, and—most importantly—make the child the centre of a story which we subsequently share with families and children alike.

These learning stories allow us to create a bridge between a child's interest in the setting and their home and allow children to share said interest, building intrinsic motivation to talk and allowing practitioners and trusted adults to scaffold existing language skills as well as introduce early literacy.

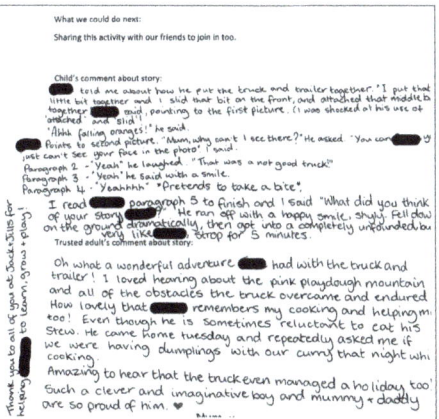

An example Learning Story

Curiosity Approach

The Curiosity Approach is an early childhood education philosophy that combines the best practices from Reggio Emilia, Montessori, Steiner, and Te Whāriki educational approaches. Founded by Lyndsey Hellyn and Stephanie Bennett, this approach emphasises creating beautiful, stimulating environments that provoke children's natural curiosity and desire to explore.[25]

The Curiosity Approach is based on child-led learning; children make their own choices and figure things out for themselves, which leads to enhanced confidence, critical thinking, and problem-solving skills. By fostering an environment in which curiosity is the driving force, this approach nurtures a love for learning, creativity, and critical thinking from a young age.

In a Curiosity Approach setting, children are given the autonomy to make choices and take risks in a safe environment. This builds their confidence and encourages independence, empowering them to take charge of their learning. The use of open-ended resources and real-world experiences fosters this, and children learn to ask questions, solve problems, and think independently, skills that are crucial for their future success.

The Curiosity Approach to early childhood education is a refreshing and innovative philosophy that places children's natural curiosity at the forefront of their learning journey. By creating environments that inspire exploration and by allowing children to lead their learning, practitioners can cultivate a lifelong love for learning, foster creativity and critical thinking, and support the holistic development of each child.[26]

Dewey

John Dewey's[27] approach to early childhood education is rooted in his broader philosophical views on democracy, experience, and the nature of learning. Dewey believed that children learn best by engaging in hands-on activities and practical experiences.

Dewey proposed that children learn through experience and that their education should be built on real-life situations and that through this style of learning, children develop independent thinking skills and are confident to experiment, and this approach subsequently nurtures a child's curiosity and fosters their desire for learning. Dewey believed that by learning hands-on, children develop their problem-solving skills, which solidifies their learning, and they can then apply the skills they've learned in the future.

Dewey's philosophy of education is grounded in pragmatism, a school of thought that emphasises the practical application of ideas and the role of experience in the formation of knowledge. Dewey believed that education should not merely prepare children for future life but should be an integral part of their present life. Learning, according to Dewey, is an active, dynamic process that involves interaction with the environment.[28] Early childhood or teaching courses which include both theory and practical elements such as placements and encourage reflection upon these experiences stem from the ideas of Dewey.

John Dewey's approach to early childhood education revolutionised the way we think about teaching and learning. By valuing the experiences and interests of children, Dewey's philosophy fosters a lifelong love of learning and prepares young minds to contribute thoughtfully and actively to society.

Dweck

In 1999, psychologist Carol Dweck published a groundbreaking book titled *Self-Theories: Their Role in Motivation, Personality, and Development*,[29] which introduced the concept of mindset and its profound implications on learning and development, particularly in early childhood education. Dweck's theory of mindset has since become a cornerstone in educational psychology, offering valuable insights into how individuals perceive and approach challenges, setbacks, and success.

At the heart of Dweck's theory is the distinction between two mindsets: the fixed mindset and the growth mindset. According to Dweck, individuals with a fixed mindset believe that their abilities and intelligence are innate and unchangeable. They tend to view challenges as threats to their self-esteem, often avoiding them to preserve their sense of competence. Conversely, those with a growth mindset see abilities and intelligence as malleable qualities that can be developed through effort, perseverance, and learning from failures.[30]

Dweck's research emphasises the critical role of mindset in shaping children's attitudes toward learning and their academic performance. During early childhood, when cognitive and social-emotional foundations are laid, the mindset children adopt significantly influences their approach to challenges and their willingness to engage in learning activities. Children with a growth mindset are more likely to embrace challenges as opportunities for growth and learning. They exhibit resilience in the face of setbacks, viewing failures as valuable learning experiences rather than reflections of their intelligence or abilities. In contrast, those with a fixed mindset may shy away from challenges, fearing failure and avoiding activities in which they might not immediately succeed.[31]

Dweck's theory has profound implications for educational practices, particularly in fostering a supportive learning environment that promotes a growth mindset. Practitioners play a pivotal role in shaping students' mindsets through their language, feedback, and instructional strategies.

Although there have been criticisms of Dweck's theory, it still offers valuable insights into the role of beliefs in shaping behaviour and academic achievement, particularly in the formative years of early childhood. By fostering a growth mindset in educational settings, practitioners can empower students to embrace challenges, persevere in the face of setbacks, and realise their full potential.

Erikson

Erik Erikson,[32] a pioneering psychologist of the 20th century, proposed a theory of human development that continues to influence practitioners, psychologists, and parents today. His theory emphasises the critical role of early childhood experiences in shaping individuals' identities, social interactions, and overall well-being.

Erikson's theory of psychosocial development suggests that individuals pass through a series of eight stages from infancy to adulthood, each characterised by a unique psychosocial crisis. These crises emerge as conflicts between inner drives and societal expectations, and successfully resolving them is essential for healthy development.[33]

Erikson's theory has significantly influenced our understanding of child development.

His focus on the social and emotional aspects of growth highlighted the importance of supportive relationships and the social environment in shaping a child's development.

Erik Erikson's theory of psychosocial development remains a cornerstone in the field of developmental psychology. By emphasising the links between individual needs and the social environment, Erikson provided a holistic framework for understanding human development. And by integrating these insights into educational practices, we as knowledgeable and nurturing practitioners can create environments that nurture holistic development and empower individuals to thrive at every stage of life.

CASE STUDY: A CHILDMINDER VIEW—NICKY GARE-MOGG

I have been a registered childminder for 24 years and worked with pre-school children for over 30 years now and so have a lot of experience.

My work ethos is entirely child led. I aim to plant as many seeds in a child's mind as I can and see which ones they want to flourish.

Following a child's interests means children will thrive and are keen to participate in the learning environment. It is my role to inspire and encourage. I provide outings and activities based around the children's interests, and I am constantly observing the children in my care to plan for all their needs in all the different areas of learning as they grow.

I strongly believe in giving young children as many different experiences/places to explore as possible and to learn as much as they can from the natural world before they start school.

In 2019 I was very fortunate to hear Dr Mine Conkbayir (award-winning author, trainer, and lecturer, Ph.D. in early childhood education and neuroscience) speak at a childminding networking conference, and her presentation really struck a chord with me and confirmed that my theories and offering as many varied and enriching experiences as possible are the best way to start a child's path in education.

Dr Conkbayir spoke about early brain development and how the research that she had been part of clearly shows that children who are ready for school are children who have been given as many different experiences as possible. Statistics have shown that nationally, speech and language development in children is behind and how childcare providers are in the ideal position to give children as many different language enriching experiences.

Dr Conkbayir talked about "lucky" children. These are not children who are from a money-rich family but children who are lucky enough to have many different language-rich experiences before they start school.

Language-rich experiences can be as simple as a trip to the shops or exploring woods or the beach for example. I work closely with other childminders in my area, which adds a real value to our trips, and we explore as many different places as possible, noticing our environment as we go. There is so much to learn from the great outdoors, and in my opinion, children should explore as much as they can before they start school.

Take this photo, for example: a simple trip to the beach with another childminder, and we are learning so much in this language-rich experience about our environment, social skills, and both fine and gross motor skills. We include numbers, shapes, and colours in addition to essential beach safety practices too.

Forest schools

Forest schools originated in Scandinavia in the 1950s. The concept was first developed in Denmark, where practitioners recognised the benefits of outdoor learning and nature-based experiences for children. Inspired by this approach, forest schools spread to other Nordic countries like Sweden and Norway. The philosophy gained international attention in the 1990s when it was introduced to the United Kingdom by a group of early childhood practitioners who visited Denmark and were impressed by the forest school model. Since then, forest schools have continued to evolve and gain popularity worldwide, with adaptations to suit different cultural and environmental contexts.[34]

Forest schools offer a unique and enriching approach to early childhood education by immersing young learners in outdoor environments, typically woodland or natural settings. This approach emphasises hands-on experiences, fostering curiosity, creativity, and resilience in children.

In forest schools, practitioners act as facilitators, encouraging exploration, problem-solving, and risk-taking in a safe and supportive environment. This holistic approach to learning recognises the inherent value of outdoor experiences in nurturing children's physical, cognitive, social, and emotional development, laying a strong foundation for lifelong learning and ecological awareness.

CASE STUDY: A TEACHER'S PERSPECTIVE— ELIZABETH LUCKHURST

During my 13 years as a teacher in primary education I have observed how an increasingly prescriptive curriculum has impacted children's recreational time both inside and outside of school. In doing so this has weakened the opportunities for experimental learning, risky play, and connection to nature for many young people.

Gaining my level 3 certificate in forest school leadership has enabled me to offer more opportunities for pupils to get outside, reconnect with nature, engage in risky play, and ultimately build self-esteem.

I have witnessed firsthand that when forest school is offered within the state sector, it can be a lifeline for many children, particularly those with additional needs. The restraints of an already squeezed school timetable, as well as a lack of funding, can be challenging, and so getting staff, management, and most importantly parents on board is crucial.

Freire

Paulo Freire, a Brazilian educator and philosopher, is renowned for his work in education and social justice. While his most famous contributions are in adult literacy and popular education, his insights have also deeply influenced early childhood education.

At the heart of Freire's pedagogy is the concept of "critical consciousness." He believed that education should not be a passive process of depositing knowledge into students' minds but rather a dynamic and transformative dialogue that empowers individuals to critically engage with the world around them.[35]

In the context of early childhood education, this means creating environments in which young children are encouraged to question, explore, and express themselves freely.

Freire's work emphasised the importance of dialogue in the learning process, viewing teachers not as authorities who impart knowledge but as facilitators who guide students in discovering knowledge for themselves.

This approach is particularly relevant in early childhood education, where children are naturally curious and eager to learn about the world. By encouraging open-ended questioning and meaningful interactions, as practitioners, we can help young children develop the skills of inquiry and critical thinking from an early age.

Freire also believed that education should not only enable individuals to understand the world but also empower them to change it. In early childhood education, this involves encouraging children to critically reflect on social issues, inequalities, and injustices and to take action to make positive changes in their communities, no matter how small.

Paulo Freire's pedagogy offers valuable insights for early childhood practitioners seeking to foster critical consciousness and social justice from the earliest stages of a child's development. By embracing principles of dialogue, respect, and empowerment, practitioners can create learning environments in which young children are encouraged to question, explore, and engage with the world in meaningful ways.

Freud

Sigmund Freud revolutionised the field of psychology with his groundbreaking theories on human behaviour and development. Among his many contributions, Freud's insights into early childhood experiences and their profound influence on individuals' lives have had a significant impact on educational practices and our understanding of human development.

At the core of Freud's theory of human development lies the concept of psychosexual stages, which he believed individuals pass through during childhood. According to Freud, these stages—oral, anal, phallic, latency, and genital—shape an individual's personality and psychological functioning. Each stage is characterised by specific conflicts and developmental tasks, and how these conflicts are resolved significantly impacts later behaviour and personality.[36]

Freud's theory has faced substantial criticism over the years. Critics argue that his ideas are unscientific, based largely on anecdotal evidence, and overly focused on sexual development.[37] Modern psychology often favours more logical approaches to understanding child development, such as those proposed by Jean Piaget or Erik Erikson.

Freud's theory of child development provides a provocative and enduring framework for understanding how early experiences shape personality. While not without its flaws, it underscores the profound impact of childhood on adult life and offers a rich, albeit contentious, narrative about the forces that drive human behaviour.

Froebel

Friedrich Froebel stands as a pioneer whose theories have significantly shaped modern approaches to early childhood education.

Froebel laid the groundwork for a holistic approach to early learning that emphasises play, creativity, and the nurturing of individuality.

Friedrich Froebel's own childhood experiences greatly influenced his views on education. As a young boy, he faced the loss of his mother and the strict discipline of his father. These early experiences and hardships fostered in him a deep empathy and understanding of the emotional needs of children, shaping his belief in the importance of a nurturing environment for their development.

Froebel is perhaps best known for inventing the concept of kindergarten, which translates to "children's garden." This revolutionary idea emerged from his belief that young children learn best through play and hands-on experiences. In 1837, he founded the first kindergarten in Bad Blankenburg, Germany, providing a space where children could engage in purposeful play, explore their surroundings, engage with nature, and develop social skills in a supportive environment which causes them to think. Central to Froebel's philosophy is the idea of "education by development." He believed that children are inherently curious and active learners who construct their understanding of the world through meaningful interactions with their environment.[38]

At the heart of Froebel's approach is the recognition of play as a fundamental aspect of childhood learning. Froebel viewed play as the primary vehicle through which children explore, experiment, and make sense of their experiences. Another key aspect of Froebel's theory is his emphasis on the unique individuality of each child. He believed that practitioners should strive to understand and support the individual needs, interests, and talents of every child, an approach and belief we know to be key in modern early years childcare and education.[39]

Friedrich Froebel's theory of early childhood education represents a significant shift in how we understand and approach the learning needs of young children. By recognising the inherent value of play, nurturing individuality, and fostering creativity, leading to a commitment to make a better world, Froebel laid the foundation for a more child-centred and holistic approach to education that so many children benefit from today.

CASE STUDY: A NURSERY SCHOOL PERSPECTIVE—GUILDFORD NURSERY SCHOOL

Guildford Nursery School embraces a Froebelian ethos, meaning that their principles and approach to early learning and development are based upon the work and ideas of Friedrich Froebel. Guildford Nursery School uses Froebel's principles to guide their learning, development, and support for all children within their setting.

Headteacher Sally Cave says, "I committed myself to Froebelian principles and pedagogy when I did my MA with Professor Tina Bruce as course director. I will always be indebted to Tina for her ongoing support, guidance and encouragement" and "Who better then to guide my work than Friedrich Froebel? A man who argued that the most important part of education was the child's first seven years. Someone who had ultimate respect for each child and their family. Someone who understood the true value of childhood and that through play, the greatest learning takes place."

Guildford Nursery School has thought carefully about how these principles can work in everyday life. They have applied them to all areas of their work and to their staff, students, and volunteers, so that everyone understands the underlying principles of this approach and the benefits, impact and why it is so important for the children, families, and educators at the setting.

The Froebelian ethos permeates all aspects of practice at the nursery school, and the following are a few practical ways this ethos is embedded:

> Freedom with guidance—children can move freely indoors and outdoors and between the two, challenge themselves, and make choices sensitively guided by educators, allowing children's uniqueness and individuality to flourish.
>
> Unity, connectedness, and community—adults build strong relationships and help link children's own lives and experiences to learning so children can connect ideas to their existing knowledge.
>
> Engaging with nature—throughout the curriculum, children are encouraged to observe nature closely and marvel at its beauty, and adults demonstrate a joyful and curious approach to nature.
>
> Learning through self-activity and reflection—children have regular opportunities to engage in many firsthand, practical experiences such as woodwork, gardening, sewing, block play, and more, with sufficient time to fully immerse themselves and revisit activities.
>
> The central importance of play—adults provide and support a wealth of exciting opportunities for play. Children are given time, space and resources which enhance this play, and parents are encouraged to value their children's play.

This Froebelian ethos is embedded in everything the nurturing and knowledgeable educators at the nursery school do and provide. Sally goes on to say, "Guildford Nursery School and Family Centre has committed to be a Froebelian organisation and I am so grateful to and proud of all the staff for their continued enthusiasm, reflective practice, and sheer hard work. With thanks to the generosity of

funding from the Froebel Trust, Guildford Nursery School and Family Centre, the Centre for Research in Early Childhood (CREC), and Ama Education Aotearoa (New Zealand) created The Froebel Partnership, and over the past three years, we have been exemplifying, documenting, and disseminating the benefits and impact of a Froebelian approach."

Gussin-Paley

Vivian Gussin-Paley, a renowned figure in the field of early childhood education, is celebrated for her profound insights into the dynamics of young children's play and communication. Central to Gussin-Paley's approach is the belief that children learn best through play and social interaction. She emphasises the importance of creating a supportive and nurturing environment in which children feel free to express themselves creatively and explore their interests.

Gussin-Paley revolutionised the way we understand child development through her innovative approaches to storytelling and dramatic play.[40] Her work emphasised the importance of children's narratives and the role of fantasy play in cognitive and social development.

Gussin-Paley advocates for the role of the teacher as a facilitator who listens attentively to children's thoughts and ideas, guiding their learning experiences while respecting their autonomy. Through her observational studies, Gussin-Paley highlights the richness of children's imaginative worlds and underscores the significance of incorporating play-based learning into the early childhood curriculum.

Gussin-Paley believed that storytelling is a fundamental method through which children make sense of their world. By narrating stories, children are not just recounting events but are actively constructing meaning and understanding complex social dynamics.

Storytelling helps children process emotions, solve problems, and develop empathy by stepping into different characters' shoes. Her contributions have greatly influenced educational practices, particularly the popular "helicopter stories" approach, inspiring practitioners to prioritise the development of social-emotional skills and fostering a deep appreciation for the unique perspectives of young learners.

Goldschmidt (see also Heuristic play and treasure baskets)

Goldschmidt's introduction of treasure baskets revolutionised the way practitioners and parents think about play for young children and emphasised the value of providing rich sensory experiences and the importance of observing children to understand their needs and interests. She believed that by providing the right environment and materials, practitioners could facilitate deep, meaningful learning without direct instruction.[41]

Helicopter Stories

"Helicopter Stories" is an educational approach in which children tell stories that are then acted out by their peers. This method was originally conceived by American educator Vivian Gussin-Paley, whose work emphasised the importance of storytelling in children's cognitive and social development. Tricia Lee has since taken Gussin-Paley's concept and tailored it to modern classrooms, making it a versatile tool that can be adapted for various educational settings.[42]

The Helicopter Stories approach is straightforward yet profoundly effective:

1. **Storytelling session:** Children are invited to dictate their stories to the educator. These stories are often short, ranging from a few sentences to a couple of paragraphs. The educator writes down the stories verbatim, honouring the child's words without corrections.
2. **Acting out stories:** Once the stories are recorded, the children gather in a circle. One by one, the stories are read aloud, and the child who authored the story gets to cast their peers in various roles. The children then act out the story with minimal props and a lot of imagination.
3. **Reflection and feedback:** After each performance, there is a moment for reflection in which children can share their thoughts and feelings about the process. This stage helps reinforce the value of listening, empathy, and collaborative learning.

There are countless benefits to this seemingly simple approach to learning that extend beyond merely developing their storytelling skills. For example, Helicopter Stories support children's development of language, confidence, social skills, empathy, and listening skills along with imagination.

Implementing Helicopter Stories in a classroom setting involves creating an environment in which children feel safe and encouraged to share their stories. Practitioners should create a safe space in which all children feel confident to share their stories and that their contributions are valued. Similarly, whilst it's important to guide the process, it is imperative that practitioners avoid altering the story and that the authenticity of the child's voice remains throughout. By fostering an environment of creativity, empathy, and confidence, helicopter stories not only enhance language and social skills but also nurture the holistic growth of young children.

HELICOPTER STORIES CASE STUDY WITH 3- AND 4-YEAR-OLDS

Cinnamon Brow School Pre-School Nursery, Warrington, Cheshire

At Cinnamon Brow nursery, we are constantly reading stories and acting them out with our children, so giving them the opportunity to invent their own seemed like a natural progression! We will wait until the children are settled within our provision before introducing helicopter stories and have found them hugely beneficial to promote many of the skills within the prime areas, as well as increasing the children's interest in reading and storytelling.

We begin by marking out a large square on the carpet using masking tape. We usually do our helicopter story sessions once a week, and each member of the nursery team has been trained to lead a small group of children, so we often act out our three groups simultaneously, as we have found this is the best way to capture the children's attention.

The adult will begin the session by asking the children to sit around the stage and to close their eyes and to breathe in deeply before opening their eyes and saying, "Welcome to the stage." This beginning ritual is important, and the more dramatic the better, as it helps to calm the children down and increases the level of anticipation! The helicopter book is then opened to reveal blank pages on which to write each story. We generally tend to follow Vivian Gussin-Paley's recommendations and write the child's name on the top of the page, telling them that this whole page belongs to them. We then give them a choice of either "One day" or "Once upon a time" to start their story and copy down word for word what the child says.

We find working in smaller groups helps to give confidence to the quieter children, and we celebrate each story, even if it is as short as, "One day, Sam!" We will then repeat the story to the child, with all the other children listening, and make a list of characters and objects which we need to match with the children. There is absolutely no recipe for the best type of story—sometimes, the more bizarre the better! We tend to go around the circle and ask each child in turn which "character" they would like to be, beginning with the author. We find this a fairer way for our younger children rather than asking the writer to choose the children to play the characters. When a child has chosen a character, we ask them to step into the stage and demonstrate how they would move/look like, and then stay sitting in the stage whilst the other characters are chosen and are acted out. After each story, we clap the characters and author and keep a record of who has and hasn't told a story.

We keep the "stage" on the carpet all week and find the children will often act out their own stories with their friends, sometimes making their own stage elsewhere in the room with masking tape and electing a child to be the scribe within play. Children sometimes come to an adult within continuous provision, asking them to write down their story, which of course we do, and will then begin with these stories during our group sessions. We have sometimes led ad-hoc helicopter story sessions within play, sometimes even using props from the room, although during our more "formal" group sessions, we tend to make our own props using children. This can be particularly fun when a child may be acting out the part of a ladder, and another has to climb the ladder to pick the apple (another child) from the apple tree (yet another child!). This approach of using children to become something other than themselves really encourages empathy

HELICOPTER STORIES

Can you guess who is a castle, aeroplane or bush? Writing and acting out our very own stories is so much fun!

and helps develop their understanding of the world around them. Very often, another child will offer suggestions as to how an apple tree should look, for example, or how a frog should jump across a lily pond!

Our nursery children absolutely love the opportunity to have a voice, and their confidence, self-esteem, and social skills have certainly improved as a result, along with their language skills and empathy for one another. I would certainly recommend considering helicopter stories for a preschool nursery setting!

Heuristic Play and Treasure Baskets

"Heuristic play" is a term derived from the Greek word "heuriskein," which means "to discover." It refers to a type of play in which children explore and learn through direct interaction with their environment. Unlike structured play, heuristic play is open-ended and child-directed, encouraging children to use their imagination and creativity. During heuristic play, children are provided with a variety of everyday objects that they can manipulate, explore, and experiment with. These objects, often referred to as "loose parts," can include items like wooden spoons, fabric scraps, pine cones, and cardboard tubes. The idea is to offer materials that are simple, non-prescriptive, and versatile, allowing children to use them in a variety of different ways.[43]

Benefits of heuristic play and treasure baskets

1. **Sensory development:** Through handling diverse objects, children engage their senses, which is crucial for brain development. They learn to differentiate between textures, weights, and shapes, enhancing their sensory perception.
2. **Fine motor skills:** Manipulating various items helps develop fine motor skills and hand–eye coordination. Picking up small objects, grasping, and moving items from one hand to another are essential for later tasks like writing.
3. **Cognitive growth:** Heuristic play encourages problem-solving and critical thinking. As children experiment with objects, they learn about cause and effect, spatial relationships, and the properties of different materials.

4. **Creativity and imagination:** With no predefined uses, the objects in heuristic play and treasure baskets invite imaginative play. A wooden spoon can become a drumstick, a bridge, or anything the child imagines, fostering creative thinking.
5. **Independence and confidence:** Allowing children to explore independently boosts their confidence and decision-making skills. They learn to trust their instincts and make choices, which is empowering.
6. **Language development:** As children explore and share their discoveries with caregivers, they are exposed to new vocabulary. Describing textures, actions, and objects enhances their language skills.[44]

Heuristic play and treasure baskets offer a powerful approach to early childhood education. By embracing child-led exploration and providing rich sensory experiences, caregivers and practitioners can foster a love of learning, creativity, and confidence in young children. These simple yet profound practices remind us that sometimes, the most effective educational tools are those that allow children to discover the world in their own unique way.

High/Scope

The High/Scope approach to early childhood care and education is a research-based child-centred philosophy that emphasises active learning, hands-on experiences, and the importance of adult–child interaction.[45] Developed by David Weikart and his colleagues in the 1960s, this approach is grounded in the belief that children learn best when they are actively engaged in meaningful activities that build upon their interests and experiences. It grew out of the Perry Preschool Study, a longitudinal research project which followed two groups of African American children from kindergarten into adulthood, some of whom had experienced a High/Scope education programme and others who did not. The children who had attended a High/Scope setting were more likely as adults to be employed, had higher earnings than the control group, and were less likely to be arrested or involved with violent crime.[46]

Key components of the high/scope approach include a carefully designed learning environment, a daily routine that incorporates time for child-initiated and adult-guided activities, and the use of the "plan-do-review" process to support children's reflection and learning. Another distinguishing element of high/scope is its problem-solving approach to conflict resolution. This strategy turns any arguments or conflicts that arise during daily practice into a problem that can be solved and resolved. It uses six steps:

1. Approach calmly
2. Acknowledge feelings
3. Gather information
4. Restate as a problem

5. Find potential solutions
6. Provide follow up support.

This approach recognises the unique strengths and developmental needs of each child and aims to foster their cognitive, social, emotional, and physical growth through purposeful play and exploration.

Hygge

Hygge, a Danish concept often translated as "cosiness," is more than just a lifestyle trend; it's a way of fostering well-being and contentment through simple pleasures and comfortable environments.[47] Whilst Hygge has gained popularity in various aspects of adult life, its principles can also profoundly impact the early years. By incorporating Hygge into early childhood education, practitioners can create warm, nurturing, and enriching learning environments that promote emotional well-being and holistic development.

Hygge (pronounced "hoo-gah") encapsulates a sense of warmth, safety, and comfort. It involves creating a welcoming atmosphere in which individuals feel relaxed and content.

In the context of early childhood, a Hygge approach simply means creating a classroom environment that feels like a second home, where children can thrive emotionally, socially, and academically.[48]

A Hygge-inspired learning environment prioritises comfort, calmness, and a sense of belonging. Following the Hygge approach to early childhood education is about more than just creating a cosy classroom; it's about fostering a holistic environment in which children feel secure, happy, and ready to learn. By embracing the principles of warmth, comfort, and community, practitioners can nurture the emotional and social development of young children, laying a strong foundation for their future growth.

The Hygge approach encourages us to slow down, appreciate the small moments, and create a learning space that feels like home, where every child can flourish.

CASE STUDY: A CHILDMINDER PERSPECTIVE

As a result of the Hygge training I undertook a few years ago, I have since taken on board the basic principles of Hygge.

Despite having previously implemented small elements of the "Hygge" idea and building my ethos upon the idea of creating a cosy, inviting, and special environment for the children in my care, I felt as a result of the training and further investigation into the Hygge principles and how this can relate and be implemented into early years settings, I then made a conscious decision to plan and create my learning environment around these principles, as I believe that creating these "special moments" and inviting, relaxing, cosy environments has incredible benefits for the children in my care in terms of their well-being, mood, behaviour and emotions.

I have always tried to limit the amount of plastic on offer, but as a result of this training, I decided to make even more of a conscious effort to do so, instead bringing in more loose parts, natural resources, soft furnishings, baskets instead of boxes, low-level lighting to create ambience, fresh flowers and lighting candles and incense as part of my everyday setup. With the physical changes I have made and the experiences I offer in order to incorporate and create a hygge-inspired environment, I have subsequently seen a significant difference in the behaviour, moods, and play of the children in my care since these changes have been implemented. They demonstrate increased levels of curiosity, higher levels of engagement and concentration, whilst also developing deeper relationships with each other, thus improving their problem-solving, critical thinking, and turn-taking as a result of this.

As a home-based childcare provider, I am exceptionally lucky to be in a position to not only have access to affordable and online CPD opportunities like the Hygge course but also to have the flexibility and freedom to implement these changes and principles almost immediately as per my new knowledge and skills and to be able to build upon these principles freely within the environment to create a calming, relaxing, and inviting play space for the children to learn and grow within.

In-The-Moment Planning

In-The-Moment-Planning (ITMP) is an educational approach developed by Anna Ephgrave[49] that emphasises spontaneous, child-initiated activities and interactions. Instead of pre-planned experiences and rigid schedules, practitioners observe children closely, identify their interests, and build learning experiences around these interests as they emerge. This approach is rooted in the belief that children learn best when they are deeply engaged in activities that are meaningful to them.[50]

In-The-Moment Planning represents a significant shift towards a more organic and child-centred approach to early childhood education. By focusing on the present moment and responding to children's immediate interests and needs, practitioners can create a vibrant, engaging, and supportive learning environment. This method relies on practitioners' ability to observe, interact, and respond to children's interests and needs in real time. Instead of adhering to a rigid curriculum, adults use their observations to create meaningful learning experiences on the spot.

Whilst ITMP offers numerous benefits, it also presents certain challenges. Practitioners need to be highly skilled in observation and interaction, requiring ongoing professional development. Additionally, balancing spontaneous learning with the need for structure and routine can be challenging. However, with careful planning and a flexible approach, these challenges can be managed effectively, with great reward.

In-The-Moment Planning is a powerful approach to early years education that prioritises children's interests and natural learning processes. By embracing spontaneity and responsiveness, practitioners can create a vibrant and engaging learning environment that nurtures children's development and love for learning.

DOI: 10.4324/9781032691367-30

CASE STUDY: A DAY NURSERY PERSPECTIVE— LITTLE RASCALS DAY NURSERY

A number of years ago, we integrated "in-the-moment planning" (ITMP) into our ethos and curriculum, enhancing our educational framework. In the past, we'd heavily relied upon short-, medium-, and long-term plans to guide the themes and activities we offered throughout the year. However, as many of our staff members engaged with high-level CPD, we became aware of ITMP, and whilst we'd always had a focus on child-led learning in the day-to-day as we focused on the children's interests and immediate needs, we had yet to apply this approach more broadly across the setting and our curriculum. This approach contrasts with traditional planning methods by prioritising spontaneity and responsiveness. Our team observe children closely, interacting and intervening at appropriate moments to extend learning experiences in real time.

To effectively implement ITMP into our setting, we initiated comprehensive training programs for all of our staff team. The training included:

1. **Ongoing professional development:** Regular meetings and reflective sessions allowed staff to discuss their experiences, share insights, and continuously refine their practice.
2. **Mentorship:** Experienced practitioners mentored newer staff, providing guidance and support as they adapted to the ITMP approach.

We then redesigned our curriculum to align with ITMP principles through:

1. **Observation and documentation:** Staff were trained to observe children's interests and document their interactions meticulously. This documentation served as a basis for planning and assessing learning.
2. **Environment as the third teacher:** The nursery environment was thoughtfully arranged to encourage exploration and discovery.

Open-ended resources and materials were readily available for children to engage with based on their interests.
3. **Flexible planning:** While long-term goals and milestones remained, the daily planning became more fluid, allowing educators to adapt activities based on real-time observations of the children's engagement.

We are huge advocates of the importance of involving parents in the educational process, and so we implemented strategies to ensure parents were informed and engaged by:

1. **Regular communication:** SMT provided regular updates on their child's interests and progress, explaining how ITMP was being used to support their learning.
2. **Workshops for parents:** Informative sessions were organised to help parents understand ITMP and how they could support their children's learning at home.
3. **Feedback mechanism:** Parents were encouraged to share their observations and insights about their children's interests and development, fostering a collaborative approach.

Since implementing ITMP, we have observed a significant increase in child engagement. Children are more enthusiastic and involved in their activities, as they are driven by their own interests and curiosity. In addition to this, ITMP allows our team to tailor learning experiences to each child's unique needs and interests. This personalised approach results in more meaningful and impactful learning experiences, supporting each child's development effectively. Similarly, shortly after this implementation, all of our team reported higher job satisfaction and a renewed passion for teaching. The flexibility and responsiveness of ITMP allowed them to be more creative and adaptive in their practice. The emphasis on parental involvement strengthened the relationship between home and nursery. Parents felt more connected to their child's learning journey and appreciated the insights and support provided by the nursery.

However, implementing ITMP was not without challenges. Staff members were initially resistant to the shift from traditional planning methods. To address this, we emphasised the benefits of ITMP through continuous training and sharing of success stories within the team. The need for meticulous documentation posed a challenge, and so we subsequently streamlined the process by adopting digital tools for easier and more efficient recording of observations. Ensuring consistent application of ITMP across all staff required ongoing monitoring and support. Regular reflective meetings and peer observations helped maintain consistency and quality.

Little Rascals owner Sharon Ashworth-Leach says, "The integration of 'in-the-moment planning' at Little Rascals Day Nursery has significantly enriched the educational experiences of both children and educators. By fostering a child-led, responsive learning environment, the nursery has created a dynamic and engaging setting that supports the holistic development of each child. Through careful planning, staff development, and strong parental involvement, Little Rascals has successfully embedded ITMP into its ethos and curriculum, setting a benchmark for innovative early years education."

Isaacs

Susan Isaacs, a renowned British psychoanalyst and educational psychologist, made significant contributions to early childhood education through her innovative and child-centric approach.

One of Isaacs's core principles is the importance of child-led learning. She believed that children are naturally curious and capable of directing their own learning experiences. Isaacs argued that when children are given the freedom to explore their interests, they become more engaged and motivated learners.[51]

This approach contrasts with traditional, adult-led education, in which the teacher dictates the learning process, which was the norm during her lifetime. In practice, child-led learning involves creating an environment rich in opportunities for exploration and discovery. Practitioners act as facilitators rather than directors, providing resources and support as children navigate their learning journeys. This method fosters independence, critical thinking, and a love for learning from an early age.

Susan Isaacs placed a strong emphasis on the role of play in child development.

She viewed play as a vital mechanism through which children make sense of the world around them, develop social skills, and process their emotions. Isaacs's research demonstrated that through imaginative play, children experiment with different roles and scenarios, helping them understand complex social dynamics and develop empathy.

To incorporate this belief into early childhood education, Isaacs advocated for ample time and space for free play. Classrooms should be equipped with a variety of materials that encourage imaginative play, such as dress-up clothes, building blocks, and art supplies. Practitioners should observe children's play to gain insights into their developmental stages and emotional well-being, using these observations to tailor support and interventions.

Isaacs recognised the integral link between emotional development and learning.

She argued that emotional well-being is foundational to a child's ability to learn effectively. According to Isaacs, children need to feel secure, understood, and valued to thrive in an educational setting. To promote emotional development, Isaacs encouraged practices that foster strong, trusting relationships between children and practitioners. This includes attentive listening, empathy, and providing consistent support. Creating a safe and nurturing environment in which children feel comfortable expressing their emotions is crucial.[52]

A cornerstone of Isaacs's approach is the use of observation to understand each child's unique needs, interests, and developmental progress. She believed that careful observation allows practitioners to tailor their support to each child rather than applying a one-size-fits-all approach. Isaacs also emphasised the importance of collaboration between practitioners and families. She believed that parents and caregivers play a crucial role in a child's education and that a strong partnership between home and school creates a more cohesive and supportive learning environment.

Susan Isaacs's approach to early childhood education remains highly relevant today.

As practitioners and policymakers continue to recognise the importance of early childhood development, Isaacs's principles offer valuable guidance. Her emphasis on child-led learning, play, emotional well-being, and individualised support aligns well with contemporary educational goals that prioritise holistic development and lifelong learning skills. Incorporating Isaacs's methods into modern educational practices involves creating environments that respect and nurture each child's innate curiosity and emotional needs.

Key Person Approach (see Attachment theory)

Among the many approaches to early childhood education, the key person approach stands out for its focus on building strong, secure relationships between children and their caregivers. This approach not only supports children's emotional and social development but also enhances their overall learning experiences. The approach is grounded in attachment theory, emphasising the importance of secure, consistent relationships in fostering a child's sense of security and belonging.

The key person approach is a method of organising early childhood care and education in which each child is assigned a specific caregiver, known as a "key person." This key person is responsible for the child's well-being, development, and learning. They act as the primary point of contact for the child and their family, building a close, trusting relationship that supports the child's individual needs and interests.[53]

The key person approach is a fundamental aspect of early childhood education, rooted in the understanding that secure, nurturing relationships are the bedrock of healthy development. By assigning each child a dedicated caregiver, this approach ensures that children receive personalised care, fostering emotional security and supporting their individual learning journeys.

Kohlberg

Laurence Kohlberg, an influential American psychologist, is best known for his groundbreaking work in moral development. His theories, although primarily focused on moral reasoning, have profound implications for early childhood education.

By understanding and integrating Kohlberg's stages of moral development, practitioners and parents can foster environments that nurture ethical thinking and behaviour from a young age. Kohlberg proposed that moral development progresses through a series of stages, each more sophisticated than the last. He categorised these stages into three main levels: pre-conventional level (up to age 9), Conventional level (early adolescence—early adulthood) and Post-conventional level (adulthood—if at all.)[54]

Early childhood, which corresponds primarily to the pre-conventional level of Kohlberg's stages, is a critical period for laying the foundation of moral understanding.

Here's how practitioners and parents can incorporate Kohlberg's principles into early childhood education:

1. **Create a respectful and safe learning environment**
    - Children learn about morality through their interactions with others. Establishing a classroom environment in which respect, safety, and care are prioritised helps children understand these concepts in practice.
2. **Promote empathy and understanding**
    - Activities that encourage children to see situations from others' perspectives can foster empathy. Role-playing and storytelling are effective tools in helping children understand different viewpoints and the reasons behind certain behaviours.

3. **Encourage moral reasoning through open dialogue**
   - Engage children in discussions about moral dilemmas appropriate for their age. Questions like "How would you feel if someone did that to you?" or "What could you do to help your friend?" promote moral reasoning.
4. **Model ethical behaviour**
   - Children learn a great deal by observing the behaviour of adults around them. Practitioners and parents should model ethical behaviour, such as honesty, kindness, and fairness, in their daily interactions.
5. **Use positive reinforcement**
   - Recognising and reinforcing positive moral behaviours can encourage children to repeat those behaviours. Praise children for acts of kindness, sharing, and fairness.

Laurence Kohlberg's theory of moral development offers valuable insights for early childhood education. By creating a respectful and empathetic learning environment, encouraging moral reasoning, and modelling ethical behaviour, practitioners and parents can nurture the moral growth of young children. Incorporating Kohlberg's principles into early childhood education is not only about teaching children what is right or wrong but also about helping them understand why it is important to care for others and society. This approach ultimately prepares children to become morally responsible and reflective individuals in their future lives.

Kohlberg also famously developed a theory of gender constancy and suggested that much like moral reasoning, children's understanding of gender also follows stages, and a child's concept of this changes over time in the same way that their thinking also changes over time. The three stages of gender development as identified by Kohlberg are gender identity/labelling, gender stability, and gender constancy.[55]

Gender identity/labelling (2–3 years) is when children are aware of gender and their own gender and can label themselves and other people as a boy or girl. However, gender is not understood as being stable, and therefore if someone changed a superficial physical characteristic, e.g. cut their hair, the child may think they have changed their gender.

Gender stability (ages 4–7) is when children begin to see gender as being a fixed concept and stable over time: girls grow to become women and boys grow to become men. Again, the full constancy of gender is not yet appreciated, as children may still believe gender can change when a person does not conform to gender roles or changes superficially, e.g. wears different clothing.

Gender constancy (age 6+) is when children are aware that gender is fixed and constant even when physical appearances change or people do not conform to gender roles. They understand that gender is a permanent concept. In Kohlberg's final stage, a child has a full appreciation of their own gender remaining constant too.

Laevers

Belgian educationalist Ferre Laevers's theory of early childhood development stands out for its focus on two fundamental pillars: well-being and involvement. This approach offers a holistic framework that emphasises the importance of emotional and psychological health as the foundation for effective learning.

Laevers developed his theory in the late 20th century, primarily through his work at the University of Leuven. His research centred around understanding what conditions facilitate optimal learning experiences for young children. Laevers identified two critical indicators of quality early childhood education: the child's well-being and their involvement in activities.

Laevers's approach to early childhood education is practical and rooted in the real-world application of his theories. It involves several key components designed to create an environment conducive to well-being and involvement, including observation and assessment, creating a supportive learning environment, responsive pedagogy, professional development, and parental involvement.[56]

Ferre Laevers's theory and approach to early childhood education offered a powerful framework for fostering well-being and involvement among young learners.

By creating environments in which children feel secure and engaged, practitioners can support holistic development and instill a lifelong passion for learning. As we continue to explore the best practices in early childhood education, Laevers's insights remind us of the importance of addressing the emotional and psychological needs of children as the foundation for their academic and personal growth.

LAEVERS SCALE CASE STUDY

Reception class at a primary school in Trafford, Greater Manchester

Using the Leuven scales helps us to identify signs of stress and understand how well our new children are settling into reception class. We score each child from 0 to 5 across the prime areas a few weeks into our autumn term and revisit them again around Christmastime. Individual observations are key, alongside other information we may have gathered about the child, which could have an impact on their learning and development, e.g. family situation, do they regularly eat breakfast, etc. We use the scores from observations to help us understand our children in a deeper way and are therefore able to design our environment to meet their individual interests and needs. We find the scales a really useful tool to ensure our children all receive the very best start on their school journey.

Loving Pedagogy

One emerging and impactful approach in the field of early childhood education is the "Loving Pedagogy" approach articulated by Tamsin Grimmer. This approach emphasises the importance of love, care, and emotional well-being in the educational process, advocating for a nurturing environment that supports holistic development.

Tamsin Grimmer's loving pedagogy is a transformative approach to early childhood education that places love, care, and emotional well-being at its core. By fostering strong relationships, creating nurturing environments, and promoting holistic development, this approach helps children thrive both emotionally and academically. As practitioners embrace the principles of loving pedagogy, they can create a more compassionate and effective educational experience for young learners, laying a solid foundation for their future growth and happiness.[57]

CASE STUDY: LOVING PEDAGOGY: A PRESCHOOL PERSPECTIVE—JACK AND JILL COMMUNITY PRESCHOOL

At Jack and Jill Community Preschool, everyone's well-being, mental health, and sense of belonging is at the core of everything we do. We firmly believe that attachment must come before attainment and that children who feel loved and cared for will feel a freedom that enables them to follow their own curiosity and explore meaningful learning opportunities, leading to them reaching their full potential.

We understand this love-and-nurture approach as one that must start from the moment we engage in relationships with prospective families. With this in mind, we have created starter packs which combine what we believe in and allow children to explore preschool long before they step (or crawl) into the actual physical space.

Our starter packs include a wooden preschool, a practitioner mini me, and two children mini mes.

These simple yet powerful play representations allow children to explore scenarios, allow families to gently ease into conversations about children starting preschool, and answer questions children might have, and they create an invisible string between home and setting where children can explore in a safe space, as well as play out things from their day at preschool once they have started to share with their significant grown-ups.

We have found that by creating a sense of belonging that starts at home, we are able to build important relationships faster, and children are usually more comfortable during their settling period and beyond.

Malaguzzi (see Reggio Emelia)

Loris Malaguzzi was an Italian educator and the founder of the Reggio Emilia approach to early childhood education, which has gained international recognition for its emphasis on child-centred learning, collaboration, and creativity.

Loris Malaguzzi's innovative approach has shaped the way we understand and practice early childhood education today. At the heart of this approach lies a deep respect for the capabilities and potential of every child. He believed that children are active participants in their own learning journey and possess an innate curiosity and creativity that should be nurtured and celebrated. Unlike traditional educational models that prioritise teacher-led instruction and a standardised curriculum, the Reggio Emilia approach views children as co-constructors of knowledge who learn best through exploration, discovery, and meaningful experiences.[58]

Malaguzzi's approach to early childhood education has had a profound impact on practitioners worldwide, inspiring a shift towards more child-centred, holistic, and inclusive practices. The Reggio Emilia philosophy celebrates the uniqueness of each child, honours their voice and agency, and promotes a deep sense of belonging and community within the classroom and beyond.

Maslow

Abraham Maslow, a renowned psychologist, introduced the concept of a hierarchy of needs, which offers valuable insights into how practitioners can support children's holistic development. His hierarchy of needs is a psychological theory that suggests humans are motivated to fulfil a series of needs, which are arranged in hierarchical order, often described as a pyramid. At the base of the pyramid are the physiological needs (e.g. food, shelter) followed by safety (e.g. feeling safe and secure), love and belonging (e.g. feeling loved), esteem (e.g. feeling worth something), and self-actualisation (e.g. meeting our potential) at the pinnacle. According to Maslow, individuals must satisfy lower-level needs before progressing to higher-order ones.[59]

Maslow's hierarchy of needs provides a valuable framework for understanding the developmental needs of young children and guiding early childhood education practices. Applying Maslow's hierarchy of needs is paramount for adequately supporting children's holistic learning in early childhood education because this hierarchy lays the foundations of children's basic needs and explicitly highlights that if a particular need is not met, a child cannot adequately progress in other areas. For example, if a child is hungry, this is an unmet need, and a practitioner would be wise to try and meet this need and feed the child before engaging in learning with them.

By addressing children's physiological, safety, belonging, esteem, and self-actualisation needs, practitioners can create nurturing environments that support holistic growth and lay the foundation for future success.

Mcmillan

The McMillan sisters, Margaret and Rachel, made significant contributions to early childhood education in the late 19th and early 20th centuries. Their approach emphasised the importance of play, health, and the environment in shaping young minds.

Born in the 19th century in Scotland, these sisters dedicated their lives to advocating for the well-being and education of young children, leaving an indelible mark on the sector to this day. Central to the McMillan sisters' philosophy was the belief that education should encompass more than just academic learning; it should nurture the physical, emotional, and social development of the child. They recognised that young children learn best through active engagement with their environment, and thus, play became a cornerstone of their educational approach.[60]

Margaret and Rachel McMillan understood the intrinsic value of play in early childhood development long before it gained widespread recognition. They saw play not merely as a pastime but as a fundamental mechanism through which children explore, experiment, and make sense of the world around them. To this end, they advocated for the provision of ample opportunities for children to engage in free, unstructured play, both indoors and outdoors.

In an era when the importance of outdoor play was often overlooked, the McMillan sisters championed the idea of nature-based education. They believed that exposure to the natural world was essential for children's physical health, emotional well-being, and cognitive development. Through outdoor activities such as gardening, nature walks, and outdoor games, children could learn valuable lessons about the environment, teamwork, and problem-solving.

The McMillan sisters also emphasised the significance of health and nutrition in early childhood education. They recognised that a child's physical well-being profoundly impacts their ability to learn and thrive. As such, they advocated for nutritious meals, proper hygiene practices, and regular health check-ups as integral components of any early childhood program.

Margaret and Rachel McMillan were also advocates for community involvement in early childhood education. They believed that parents, teachers, and the wider community should work collaboratively to create nurturing environments that support children's holistic development. By fostering strong partnerships between schools, families, and local organisations, they sought to create a network of support that extended beyond the classroom walls.[61]

In a time when early childhood education was still in its infancy, Margaret and Rachel McMillan emerged as trailblazers whose progressive ideas paved the way for future generations of practitioners. Through their advocacy for play, nature-based learning, health promotion, and community engagement, they laid the foundation for a more holistic approach to early childhood education—one that remains as relevant and inspiring today as it was over a century ago.

Montessori

The Montessori approach stands out in early childhood education as a beacon of individualised learning, nurturing the innate curiosity and potential of each child. Developed by Dr Maria Montessori in the early 20th century, this approach has transcended time and culture, offering a unique blend of philosophy and methodology that continues to shape early childhood education worldwide.

At the heart of the Montessori philosophy lies a deep respect for the child as a curious, capable, and active learner. Dr Montessori believed that children possess an innate drive to explore and understand the world around them, and it is through purposeful engagement with their environment that they construct knowledge and develop essential skills.[62]

Central to the Montessori approach is the concept of the prepared environment. Classrooms are thoughtfully designed to encourage independence, exploration, and discovery. Materials are carefully selected to be developmentally appropriate and sensorially engaging, inviting children to learn through hands-on exploration and manipulation.

The key principles of the Montessori approach are:

- **Child-led learning:** In a Montessori classroom, the child takes the lead in their learning journey. Teachers serve as guides, observing each child's interests, strengths, and challenges and providing individualised support and encouragement. This fosters a sense of ownership and autonomy, empowering children to explore topics at their own pace and in their own unique way.
- **Mixed-age groupings:** Montessori classrooms typically include children spanning a range of ages, fostering a sense of community

and collaboration. Older children serve as mentors and role models for younger peers, while younger children benefit from observing and learning from their older counterparts. This multi-age dynamic promotes social skills, empathy, and a deeper understanding of concepts as children engage in peer-to-peer teaching and learning.
- **Concrete learning materials:** Montessori materials are meticulously designed to appeal to the senses and facilitate hands-on exploration. From the iconic Montessori pink tower to the golden bead materials for maths, each material is carefully crafted to isolate and emphasise specific concepts, allowing children to move from the concrete to the abstract with ease.
- **Freedom within limits:** While freedom is a cornerstone of the Montessori philosophy, it is not a free-for-all. Children are given the freedom to choose their activities, work at their own pace, and explore their interests, but within a framework of clear boundaries and expectations. This balance of freedom and structure provides children with a sense of security and autonomy while fostering self-discipline and responsibility.

The Montessori approach to early childhood education and its relevance even today represents a shift in how we view and support children's learning and development. By honouring the child as a capable and curious individual, Montessori education empowers children to reach their full potential, both academically and personally, with knowledgeable and supportive practitioners at its forefront.

Parten

Mildred Parten, an American sociologist, conducted groundbreaking research in the 1930s on the social behaviour of preschool children.[63] Her work laid the foundation for understanding how children engage with their peers and the developmental stages they undergo in social interaction.[64]

Parten's theory outlines six stages of social play, ranging from solitary play to cooperative play.

Each stage represents a different level of social interaction, and children typically progress through these stages as they grow and develop.[65]

1. **Unoccupied play:** At this stage, children engage in seemingly aimless movements or behaviours. They might wander around, fiddle with objects, or watch others play without actively participating.
2. **Solitary (independent) play:** Solitary play involves children playing alone, often immersed in their own activities and interests. They may interact with toys or engage in imaginative play independently of others.
3. **Onlooker play:** In this stage, children observe others playing but do not actively engage with them. They may show interest in what their peers are doing, ask questions, or make comments, but they refrain from joining in the play themselves.
4. **Parallel play:** Parallel play marks the beginning of social interaction, in which children play alongside each other without significant interaction. They may use similar toys or engage in similar activities, but they do not actively engage with one another.

5. **Associative play:** Associative play involves more interaction among children. While they may pursue different activities, they share materials, ideas, and conversation. There is a sense of cooperation and a willingness to engage with others, although play remains somewhat unstructured.
6. **Cooperative play:** The highest level of social play, cooperative play, involves organised and coordinated interaction among children. They work together towards a common goal, follow rules, take on different roles, and resolve conflicts collaboratively. This stage fosters teamwork, communication, and social skills essential for later life.

Understanding Parten's stages of social play is invaluable for practitioners working with young children. By recognising the developmental progression of social behaviours, they can create environments that support and encourage healthy social interaction.

Parten's theory provides valuable insights into the social development of young children and offers a framework for promoting healthy social interactions in early childhood education settings. By understanding the stages of social play and implementing appropriate strategies, practitioners can create nurturing environments in which children can thrive socially and emotionally.

Pavlov

When we think of the name Pavlov, most minds instinctively conjure images of salivating dogs and ringing bells. While Ivan Pavlov's groundbreaking work in classical conditioning has left an indelible mark on the field of psychology, its implications for early childhood development are equally important.

Pavlov's experiments, conducted in the late 19th and early 20th centuries, focused on understanding the mechanisms of learning through conditioning. His most famous experiment involved ringing a bell just before presenting food to dogs. Over time, the dogs began to salivate at the sound of the bell alone, even when food was not present. This phenomenon, known as classical conditioning, demonstrated how associations between stimuli could shape behaviour.[66]

We can also apply these principles from Pavlov's experiments to early childhood education. For example, we may get a bib for a baby and they get excited, knowing they are going to have some milk or food.

At the core of Pavlov's theory is the idea that learning occurs through the association of stimuli. In the context of early childhood, this principle underscores the importance of environmental influences on a child's development. Just as Pavlov's dogs learned to associate the bell with food, children learn to associate various stimuli with experiences, emotions, and actions. This is about unconscious or automatic learning, and these early associations lay the foundation for future learning and behaviour.

Similarly, Pavlov's experiments highlight the significant role of the environment and routine in shaping behaviour. For young children, the environment encompasses everything from the physical surroundings to social interactions and experiences. Every interaction, whether with caregivers, peers, or objects, contributes to the child's cognitive and emotional development. Understanding the power of environmental stimuli allows parents, practitioners, and caregivers to create nurturing and stimulating environments conducive to healthy development.[67]

Pavlov's work underscores the potential for behaviour modification through conditioning. While his experiments primarily focused on involuntary responses, such as salivation, the principles of conditioning can be applied to a wide range of behaviours in children (although arguably, this poses debate within our sector). By reinforcing positive behaviours and discouraging negative ones, caregivers can help shape children's actions and attitudes in desirable ways. Consistent reinforcement and repetition play crucial roles in this process, as does learning through routines.

Pedagogy

"Pedagogy" is a term used within early childhood education, and it stems from the Greek word *"paidagogos,"* meaning "to lead a child." It is often used in conjunction with "teaching," explaining an educational approach in terms of everything we do and provide for children and the rationale of why we do it that way. Within early childhood, our pedagogy or pedagogical approach includes our whole ethos and the way we do things, the relationships we foster, the teaching strategies we employ, and the way we create our learning environments.[68]

There are a number of different pedagogical approaches within early childhood education, many of which are listed in this book, for example, Froebel, Montessori, Steiner, Reggio Emilia, curiosity approach, forest/beach schools, Te Whāriki, high/scope, mosaic approach, in-the-moment planning, slow pedagogy, loving pedagogy, and trauma-informed practice. Some of these are approaches which encompass their whole provision and defines the ethos of the setting and are therefore mutually exclusive, whereas a few can be adopted alongside others. Defining our pedagogical approach and discussing it as a team is important because our pedagogy shapes our children and our approach to supporting and caring for them.

Piaget (see also Schema theory)

Jean Piaget, a Swiss psychologist, is renowned for his groundbreaking work in child development. His theory provides a framework for understanding how children actively construct their understanding of the world. Central to Piaget's theory is the idea that children progress through distinct stages of cognitive development, each characterised by unique ways of thinking and understanding.[69]

Piaget proposed four main stages of cognitive development:

1. **Sensorimotor stage (birth to 2 years):** During this stage, infants learn about the world through their senses and actions, e.g. learning through firsthand experiences. They develop object permanence, which is the understanding that objects continue to exist even when they are out of sight. Infants also begin to coordinate their sensory experiences with motor actions, laying the foundation for more complex cognitive processes.
2. **Preoperational stage (2 to 7 years):** In this stage, children engage in symbolic play and develop language skills, such as playing with a brick as if it were a mobile phone. However, their thinking is still egocentric, meaning they struggle to understand the perspectives of others. They also exhibit animistic thinking, attributing human-like qualities to inanimate objects, for example, playing with a toy dinosaur and making it talk or cry. Conservation tasks, such as understanding that the quantity of a substance remains the same despite changes in shape or arrangement, are challenging for children in this stage.
3. **Concrete operational stage (7 to 11 years):** Children in this stage demonstrate more logical thinking and begin to grasp concepts such as conservation and reversibility. They can solve problems

using concrete objects and understand the concept of conservation, for example, recognising that 10 items always amount to 10, even if they are arranged in a different pattern or consist of different objects. However, their thinking is still tied to concrete, tangible experiences, limiting their ability to reason abstractly.
4. **Formal operational stage (11 years and older)**: During this final stage, individuals develop the ability to think abstractly and hypothetically. They can engage in deductive reasoning and consider multiple perspectives on complex issues. This stage marks the attainment of adult-like cognitive abilities, allowing individuals to engage in higher-level thinking and problem-solving.

Piaget's theory of early childhood development revolutionised our understanding of how children think and learn. By recognising the distinct stages of cognitive development and the role of experience in shaping children's understanding, practitioners and caregivers can create environments that support children's growth and development to their fullest potential.[70]

Pikler approach

At its core, the Pikler approach, named after paediatrician Dr Emmi Pikler (1902–1984), emphasises respect for the child as an autonomous individual, acknowledging their inherent competency and agency from the earliest stages of life. Dr Pikler believed that infants and young children are active participants in their own development, capable of initiating and directing their learning experiences within a supportive environment.[71]

The key principles of the Pikler approach include:

1. **Trust in the child:** Central to the Pikler approach is the belief that children develop best when they are provided with a secure, trusting relationship with their caregivers. This trust forms the foundation for healthy attachment and emotional well-being.
2. **Freedom of movement:** Dr Pikler recognised the importance of allowing infants and young children the freedom to move and explore their surroundings at their own pace. This includes providing ample time for uninterrupted play and opportunities for self-directed movement, such as crawling, climbing, and grasping objects.
3. **Observation and responsive caregiving:** Caregivers in a Pikler-inspired environment are encouraged to observe children closely, tuning into their cues and signals and responding sensitively to their needs. This attentive approach fosters a deep understanding of each child's unique temperament, preferences, and developmental milestones.
4. **Scaffolding learning:** Rather than imposing predetermined activities or goals, the Pikler approach advocates for scaffolding learning experiences based on each child's current abilities and interests.

Caregivers act as facilitators, offering gentle guidance and support as children engage in self-directed exploration and problem-solving.
5. **Respect for rhythms and rituals:** Dr Pikler emphasised the importance of respecting children's natural rhythms and establishing predictable routines within the caregiving environment. Consistent daily rituals, such as feeding, diapering, and nap times, provide children with a sense of security and stability, fostering a sense of trust and well-being.

In a world in which the pace of life seems to accelerate with each passing day, the Pikler approach serves as a poignant reminder of the importance of slowing down, tuning in to the needs of children, and fostering deep, meaningful connections based on mutual respect and trust.

Professional Love

Professional Love, as conceptualised by Dr Jools Page, refers to the expression of love in a professional context in which early childhood practitioners provide care and education. This approach balances emotional warmth and professional boundaries, ensuring that children feel secure, valued, and supported while maintaining an environment conducive to learning and development.[72]

The core principles of Page's Professional Love approach are:

1. **Emotional warmth and security:** Professional love advocates for the creation of a warm, affectionate environment in which children feel safe and secure. Emotional warmth is crucial for young children because it fosters a sense of belonging and trust, which are foundational for effective learning and social development.
2. **Professional boundaries:** While advocating for love and affection, this approach also emphasises the importance of maintaining professional boundaries. Practitioners are trained to show care and empathy in a manner that is appropriate and respectful, ensuring that the emotional needs of children are met without overstepping personal boundaries.
3. **Holistic development:** The approach recognises the interconnectedness of emotional, social, and cognitive development. By integrating professional love, practitioners support the holistic growth of children, addressing their emotional needs alongside their educational and developmental milestones.
4. **Ethical considerations:** Professional love involves a strong ethical framework in which practitioners are mindful of their influence and power dynamics in the relationship with children. This ensures that

the affectionate behaviour remains ethical and beneficial to the child's development.

The importance of Professional Love in early childhood education must not be overlooked. Professional Love in the context of early childhood builds trust, supports emotional resilience, and creates a positive learning environment, which subsequently enhances a child's learning outcomes.

Jools Page's Professional Love approach offers a nuanced and compassionate framework for early childhood education. By fostering emotional warmth while maintaining professional boundaries, this approach supports the holistic development of children, building the foundation for lifelong learning and well-being. For practitioners, embracing professional love can transform settings and classrooms into nurturing environments where every child feels valued, respected, and loved.

Reggio Emelia

Originating in the small Italian town of Reggio Emilia after World War II, this educational philosophy was developed by Loris Malaguzzi and parents in the surrounding villages. Its core principles focus on the potential of children, the importance of community and collaboration, and the role of the environment as a crucial component in learning.

At the heart of the Reggio Emilia approach is a profound respect for children. It views children as competent, curious, and capable of constructing their own knowledge. This principle challenges traditional views that see children as empty vessels to be filled with information. Instead, children are seen as active participants in their learning journey.

Teachers and practitioners in Reggio Emilia settings act as co-learners and collaborators rather than authoritative figures. They facilitate learning by observing, listening, and engaging with children's ideas. Teachers document children's work and use these observations to guide further learning and exploration.[58]

The learning environment in Reggio Emilia schools is carefully designed to be welcoming, aesthetically pleasing, and filled with natural light. Spaces are organised to encourage exploration, communication, and collaboration. Materials are thoughtfully selected to provoke curiosity and creativity. The environment itself is considered an essential component of learning, influencing how children interact and learn.

Learning in Reggio Emilia is project based, allowing children to explore topics of interest in depth. Projects can be short term or long term and are driven by children's questions and curiosities. This approach fosters a deeper understanding of subjects and encourages children to think critically and solve problems creatively.

Documentation is a critical element of the Reggio Emilia approach. Practitioners capture children's learning processes through photographs, videos, and written observations. This documentation is displayed throughout the classroom and shared with children and parents. It serves multiple purposes: it makes learning visible, helps teachers reflect on their practice, and engages parents in their children's education.

Unlike traditional education systems with a fixed curriculum, the Reggio Emilia approach follows a flexible and emergent curriculum. Topics are not predetermined but emerge from children's interests and enquiries. This flexibility allows for a more personalised learning experience, adapting to the needs and passions of each child.[73]

The Reggio Emilia approach to early childhood education is a powerful and holistic educational philosophy that places children at the centre of their learning experience. By valuing the potential and competence of children, involving the community, and creating beautiful and inspiring environments, this approach fosters a love of learning and nurtures the development of well-rounded, curious, and capable individuals.

CASE STUDY: A CHILDMINDER'S PERSPECTIVE

I have been a childminder for over 10 years and am passionate about early childhood education. I decided to implement the Reggio Emilia approach in my setting to enhance the learning experiences of the children I care for, as the philosophy and beliefs of this approach are consistent with my own beliefs on how children learn best.

The principles of respect, responsibility, and community through exploration and discovery in a supportive and enriching environment are something I wholeheartedly believe in, and I love that this approach places emphasis on the child as a competent, capable, and curious individual who learns best through self-directed play and exploration. The environment plays a crucial role in the Reggio Emilia approach, often referred to as the "third teacher." To align my setting with this principle, I have made several changes:

I reorganised the playroom to create a more open and inviting space that encourages exploration. Introducing natural materials, like wooden blocks, stones, and shells, to create a connection with nature. The environment was designed to be flexible, allowing children to move items and create their own play scenarios.

In addition to this, I have introduced documentation panels in the playroom where children's artwork, photographs, and notes about their activities were displayed. This not only makes the children feel valued but also helps me reflect on the children's interests and learning progress. I have also utilised the garden as an extension of the indoor learning environment, creating a small vegetable patch where children could plant, water, and watch their plants grow, fostering a connection with nature and responsibility.

Scaffolding (see Bruner and Vygotsky)
Schema theory

In early childhood education, understanding how children learn and develop is crucial for creating effective teaching strategies. One influential framework that offers insights into this process is schema theory. This theory, which has roots in cognitive psychology, emphasises the role of schemas—mental structures that help individuals organise and interpret information. By exploring schema theory, practitioners can better understand how young children interact with their environment, process new information, and develop essential cognitive skills.

Schema theory was first introduced by British psychologist Frederic Bartlett in the early 20th century and later expanded by psychologists such as Jean Piaget. Schemas are cognitive frameworks or mental structures that help individuals organise and interpret information based on past experiences and knowledge. These structures enable us to understand and predict the world around us, making it easier to learn and recall information.[74]

In the context of early childhood education, schemas are patterns of repeated behaviour that children exhibit as they explore their environment and make sense of their experiences. These patterns, or schemas, are essential for cognitive development and learning, providing a foundation for acquiring new knowledge and skills.[75]

Children often display various types of schemas as they interact with their surroundings. Some common schemas observed in early childhood include:

- **Trajectory schema:** This involves activities that focus on moving objects or the child's own body along a path, such as throwing balls, sliding, or running.

- **Rotation schema:** Children with this schema are fascinated by things that turn, like wheels, spinning tops, or rotating their own bodies.
- **Enclosure schema:** This includes activities in which children create enclosures or boundaries, such as building fences with blocks, playing in boxes, or drawing circles around objects.
- **Transporting schema:** Children exhibiting this schema enjoy moving objects from one place to another, often using containers, bags, or their hands.
- **Connection schema:** This involves linking things together, such as connecting train tracks, joining blocks, or tying things together.[76]

Understanding these schemas helps practitioners recognise the underlying cognitive processes at work and tailor their teaching strategies to support and extend children's learning. Integrating schema theory into early childhood education involves creating an environment that supports and encourages the natural exploration and development of schemas. This could be done in a number of ways, including observations and assessments, the design of the physical learning environment, collaborative learning, and scaffolded learning.

Schema theory offers valuable insights into how young children learn and develop. By understanding and applying this theory, practitioners can create enriched learning environments that support and extend children's natural exploration and cognitive development. Recognising and nurturing schemas in early childhood education not only enhances individual learning experiences but also promotes a lifelong love of discovery and learning. (See also Athey and Piaget for more.)

Skinner

B.F. Skinner, a prominent figure in the field of psychology, made significant contributions to our understanding of behaviour through his theory of operant conditioning. His work has had a profound impact on various fields, including education. In early childhood education, Skinner's principles offer valuable insights and practical strategies for fostering positive behaviour and effective learning.

At the heart of Skinner's theory is the concept of operant conditioning, which focuses on how consequences influence behaviour. Skinner identified three types of responses that can follow behaviour:

1. **Positive reinforcement:** Introducing a pleasant stimulus to increase the likelihood of a behaviour being repeated, for example, giving a child a sticker if they are kind.
2. **Negative reinforcement:** Removing an unpleasant stimulus to increase the likelihood of a behaviour being repeated, for example, telling a child they do not have to tidy up because they listened well during the story.
3. **Punishment:** Introducing an unpleasant stimulus or removing a pleasant one to decrease the likelihood of a behaviour being repeated, for example, telling a child they cannot play with the playdough because they shouted.

Skinner's principles can be applied in early childhood education to promote desirable behaviours and enhance learning. However, his ideas around rewards and punishment have been critiqued as unhelpful because they focus on obedience and compliance rather than moral understanding.

Skinner also introduced the concept of shaping, which involves reinforcing successive approximations of a desired behaviour. In early childhood education, this can be particularly useful for teaching complex skills by breaking them down into smaller, manageable steps.[77]

Skinner highlighted the importance of reinforcement schedules in maintaining behaviour. Continuous reinforcement (reinforcing every correct response) is useful for establishing new behaviours, while intermittent reinforcement (reinforcing some but not all correct responses) is more effective for maintaining established behaviours. By understanding the principles of operant conditioning, practitioners can help children develop self-regulation and autonomy. Encouraging children to recognise the consequences of their actions and make choices based on these understandings can foster independence.

B.F. Skinner's theory of operant conditioning provides a framework for understanding and influencing behaviour, which is often used in early childhood education. It is in contrast to a more relational approach in which adults teach children right from wrong through role-modelling, scaffolding tasks, and emotion coaching.

Slow Pedagogy

In a world increasingly obsessed with speed and efficiency, the concept of "slow" has taken on a revolutionary significance in various fields, from food to travel. In the realm of early childhood education, the slow movement has found a profound expression through the work of Alison Clark and Jo Albion, who advocate for "slow pedagogy."[78]

Slow pedagogy is a thoughtful, reflective approach to education that counters the prevalent culture of hurry and standardised benchmarks. It encourages practitioners to slow down and focus on the quality of interactions and experiences rather than the quantity of activities or the speed of progress. This philosophy aligns with the broader slow movement, which values mindfulness, intentionality, and depth over speed and superficiality.

Slow pedagogy offers a refreshing and profoundly effective approach to early childhood learning and development. By slowing down, focusing on deep engagement, and prioritising the child's natural pace of learning, practitioners can foster a more enriching and supportive environment for young learners. This method not only enhances cognitive and emotional development but also builds a stronger, more connected community of learners, practitioners, and families. In an era in which speed often trumps quality, embracing the principles of slow pedagogy can lead to more meaningful and lasting educational outcomes.

Steiner

Rudolf Steiner's philosophy of education, known as Waldorf education, offers a unique and holistic approach to early childhood education. Rooted in anthroposophy, Steiner's educational model emphasises the developmental stages of children, the importance of imagination, and the integration of artistic, practical, and academic activities.[79]

Steiner's approach focuses on nurturing the physical, emotional, intellectual, and spiritual aspects of a child. Education is seen as an organic process that supports the growth of the whole child, ensuring a balanced development.[80]

According to Steiner, childhood development occurs in three seven-year phases:

- **First seven years (0–7):** Emphasis on physical development and sensory experiences. The environment is designed to be warm, secure, and homelike, encouraging free play and exploration.
- **Second seven years (7–14):** Focus shifts to imaginative and emotional development. Storytelling, arts, and hands-on activities are central, nurturing creativity and social skills.
- **Third seven years (14–21):** Intellectual and moral development come to the forefront. Critical thinking, abstract reasoning, and ethical considerations are cultivated.

Waldorf kindergartens are designed to be warm, nurturing, and aesthetically pleasing. Natural materials, handmade toys, and a home-like atmosphere create a sense of comfort and security. The curriculum is flexible and adapts to the needs of the children. It includes storytelling, puppetry, singing, painting, baking, gardening, and other hands-on activities. Festivals and seasonal celebrations are also integral, providing cultural richness and a sense of community. Waldorf education encourages strong parent–teacher partnerships. Parents are often involved in school activities, festivals, and regular meetings to ensure a cohesive and supportive community for the children.[81]

Steiner's method recognises that each child is unique. By focusing on the whole child and providing a nurturing environment, Waldorf education allows children to develop their strengths and interests. The emphasis on arts and play fosters creativity, imagination, and a love for learning. Children learn to think creatively and approach problems with innovative solutions. The holistic approach supports emotional intelligence and social skills. Through group activities and collaborative play, children learn empathy, cooperation, and communication. Waldorf education's integration of nature and seasonal rhythms helps children develop a deep respect and appreciation for the natural world.

Rudolf Steiner's approach to early childhood education offers a rich, holistic, and nurturing environment that fosters the overall development of children. By emphasising creativity, imagination, and a deep connection to nature, Waldorf education prepares children not just academically but as well-rounded individuals ready to navigate the complexities of life. For parents and practitioners seeking an alternative to conventional education, Steiner's methods provide a timeless and effective framework for early childhood learning.

Te Whāriki

Originating from New Zealand, Te Whāriki, which translates to "the woven mat," symbolises the interconnectedness of all aspects of learning and development in a child's life. Developed in the 1990s, this approach emphasises the importance of fostering not just academic skills but also social, emotional, cultural, and physical well-being.[82]

At the heart of Te Whāriki lies a deep respect for cultural diversity and the recognition of the unique identity of each child. The framework acknowledges the significance of indigenous knowledge and values, honouring the rich tapestry of cultural backgrounds within New Zealand and beyond. Practitioners are encouraged to weave cultural perspectives into every aspect of the learning environment, from curriculum planning to daily routines, ensuring that children feel a sense of belonging and pride in their heritage.[83]

Te Whāriki views children as competent and capable learners, capable of constructing their understanding of the world through meaningful interactions and experiences. Rather than focusing solely on cognitive development, the framework advocates for a holistic approach that nurtures all dimensions of a child's being—cognitive, social, emotional, physical, and spiritual. Learning is seen as a dynamic process that occurs in diverse contexts and is influenced by relationships with others, both peers and adults.

Central to Te Whāriki is the concept of "ako," which highlights the reciprocal nature of teaching and learning. Practitioners are encouraged to adopt a collaborative approach in which they engage in respectful and responsive relationships with children, families, and communities. By fostering strong connections and partnerships, practitioners create a supportive learning environment in which children feel safe, valued, and empowered to explore and express themselves.

Play is considered the cornerstone of learning in Te Whāriki, providing children with opportunities to explore, experiment, and make sense of their world. Practitioners facilitate play experiences that are open ended, child directed, and rich in possibilities, allowing for creativity, imagination, and problem-solving skills to flourish.

Te Whāriki offers a flexible and responsive curriculum framework that adapts to the diverse needs, interests, and strengths of individual children. Practitioners are encouraged to observe, assess, and document children's learning journeys, using this information to plan meaningful and relevant learning experiences.

Te Whāriki offers a holistic and culturally responsive approach to early childhood education that honours the unique identities and diverse backgrounds of every child. By weaving together the threads of culture, play, relationships, and learning, practitioners create a nurturing and empowering environment in which children can thrive and reach their full potential.

Trauma-Informed Practice or Trauma-Responsive Practice

Trauma, in the context of early childhood, encompasses a wide range of experiences, from exposure to violence or substance abuse within the family to the effects of poverty and displacement. Sometimes described as adverse childhood experiences (ACEs), these experiences can disrupt a child's sense of safety and security, leading to heightened stress responses and challenges in emotional regulation.[84]

Moreover, trauma can significantly impact the development of attachment—the deep emotional bond between a child and their primary caregiver. Secure attachment is crucial for healthy social and emotional development, providing a foundation for trust, empathy, and self-esteem. However, trauma can disrupt this attachment bond, leading to insecure attachment styles characterised by anxiety, avoidance, or ambivalence.

At the heart of trauma-informed or trauma-responsive practice lies relational practice—a commitment to building trusting, empathetic relationships with each child. In an early years setting, relational practice involves creating a nurturing environment in which children feel valued, respected, and understood. Practitioners strive to establish secure attachments with their children, serving as consistent sources of support and guidance.

In addition to relational practice, trauma-informed early years settings prioritise creating attachment-aware environments that promote a sense of safety and belonging. These settings are characterised by warmth, predictability, and sensory-rich experiences that engage children's senses and foster emotional regulation.[85]

Attachment-aware schools and settings integrate strategies such as structured routines, clear boundaries, and positive reinforcement to create a sense of stability and security. Moreover, practitioners receive training in recognising and responding to signs of trauma, equipping them with the tools to support children's emotional well-being effectively.

In the journey through early childhood, every interaction shapes the developing brain and lays the groundwork for future relationships. Trauma-informed practice in the early years recognises the profound impact of adverse experiences on children's development and seeks to mitigate these effects through relational practice and attachment-aware settings.

Treasure Baskets (see also Heuristic play)

Treasure baskets are a key component of heuristic play, particularly for infants and toddlers. Introduced by Elinor Goldschmidt, treasure baskets are collections of natural and everyday objects presented to young children to explore using their senses. Goldschmidt's work emphasised the importance of sensory experiences in early development.[86]

A treasure basket typically contains a variety of items with different textures, shapes, sizes, and weights. Examples include metal spoons, wooden blocks, natural sponges, and pieces of fabric. The objects are chosen to stimulate the senses and provoke curiosity. The basket is placed within reach of a sitting baby, allowing them to choose, handle, and investigate the items at their own pace. (See Heuristic play for more.)

Vygotsky

In the realm of educational theory, Lev Vygotsky's[87] ideas have profoundly influenced how we understand the learning process, particularly in early childhood education. Central to Vygotsky's framework is the concept of the zone of proximal development (ZPD), a notion that sheds light on the dynamic interplay between a child's current abilities and their potential for growth with the right support and guidance.

At the core of Vygotsky's theory is the belief that social interaction plays a pivotal role in cognitive development. Unlike some other theories that emphasise individual exploration and discovery, Vygotsky posited that learning is inherently social and occurs through collaboration and interaction with more knowledgeable others, such as teachers, parents, or peers.[88]

Practitioners who embrace this framework understand the importance of scaffolding—providing the necessary support and guidance to help children navigate their ZPD and reach their full potential. Rather than simply imparting knowledge, practitioners act as facilitators, guiding children through challenging tasks, asking probing questions, and providing timely feedback.

In Vygotsky's theory of early childhood education, we find a powerful framework that emphasises the interconnectedness of social interaction, cognitive development, and cultural context. By understanding and applying the principles of Vygotskian education, practitioners can create rich learning environments in which every child has the opportunity to thrive and reach their full potential.

Waldorf (see Steiner)
Winnicott

Donald Winnicott proposed that children sometimes have an attachment to their possessions, and this adds to their sense of self and identity.[89] We see this when a child may have an attachment to a special object, for example, a teddy, dummy, or muslin cloth. These are described as "transitional objects." These possessions help the child feel safe and secure, and Winnicott suggested some children may need these objects for a period of time. Allowing the child access to this object will eventually contribute to their physical and emotional independence.

He also coined the term "good-enough mother," which is when a parent responds to their child consistently and sensitively in a warm and loving way, adapting to their needs appropriately. Being "good enough" is in contrast to being "perfect" and allows for parents to occasionally make mistakes. Being a perfect parent might mean they expect their child to never cry or get angry or upset, whereas in reality, these emotions are natural. Being good enough means responding quickly and sensitively to a child and accepting that they will sometimes experience these emotions. When parents respond to their child in this way, the child learns to trust their parent, and it adds to their secure attachment. We can strive to be "good enough" practitioners in our daily interactions with children, responding sensitively to children.

CASE STUDY: A CHILDMINDER'S PERSPECTIVE

Georgia was given a doll for her first birthday and named her Baby. From that moment, Baby became a large part of her life. She took Baby everywhere, so it stood to reason that when Georgia joined my childminding setting, Baby did too.

Georgia and Baby were inseparable. When Georgia was tired, she needed to cuddle Baby and often asked for her. I needed to very carefully look after Baby and make sure she joined us for outings and such, ensuring she didn't get left behind or lost. Baby became part of our setting, and the other children would also refer to Baby, saving her a place at the table or inviting her to join us to listen to a story.

Georgia used baby as a transitional object. She was emotionally connected to Baby and treated her like a member of the family. She also relied on her for comfort, particularly when she was in an unfamiliar place. So Baby came to the library with us, to toddler groups, and on all our adventures. As her childminder, I recognised the significance of Baby in her life and saw, firsthand, how an emotional connection to an object can help a child feel more secure.

I understand that Georgia took Baby to school for her school visit, and it is my hope that the teachers acknowledged and recognised the importance of Baby in Georgia's life as a transitional object.

Zone of Proximal Development (see also Vygotsky)

The Zone of Proximal Development (ZPD) was developed by Vygotsky and refers to the gap between what a child can do independently and what they can achieve with the guidance and support of a more knowledgeable other. In essence, the ZPD represents the "sweet spot" of learning, where challenges are neither too easy nor too difficult but perfectly matched to the child's current level of development.[90]

Practitioners can identify this zone for each child and tailor their instructions accordingly, offering challenges just beyond their current capabilities. This is often referred to as scaffolding a child's learning (see Bruner).

Conclusion of Part 1

I hope the first section has been useful in giving you a brief overview of many of the key theories and approaches that have shaped early years education. Following is a list of further ideas and suggestions of places to look and websites linked with each of the definitions provided.

Further Reading and Resources

Ainsworth

https://www.sticksandstoneseducation.com.au/blogs/educators-notebook-the-early-years-edition/theorist-in-the-spotlight-mary-ainsworth

Anti-racist practice

https://www.theblacknurserymanager.com/
Louis, S., and Betteridge, H. (2024). *Let's Talk About Race in the Early Years*. Abingdon: Routledge.

Athey

Arnold, C. (ed.). (2022). *Schemas in the Early Years: Exploring Beneath the Surface Through Observation and Dialogue*. Abingdon: Routledge.
https://www.nurseryworld.co.uk/content/features/early-years-pioneers-chris-athey/

Attachment theory

https://eyfs.info/articles.html/general/attachment-theory-and-the-key-person-approach-r64/#:~:text=Ainsworth%20found%20that%20there%20were,the%20departure%20or%20return%20of
Video—https://www.sirenfilms.co.uk/library/attachment-feeling-safe-and-secure/

Bandura

https://www.allanarobinson.com/early-childhood-theories-albert-bandura/
https://www.parenta.com/2018/07/01/childrens-social-learning-some-insights-into-the-ideas-of-albert-bandura/

Bavolek

Bradbury, A. (2022). Stephen Bavolek. In Bradbury, A., and Swailes, R. (eds.), *Early Childhood Theories Today*. London: Learning Matters.
https://www.eymatters.co.uk/product/early-childhood-theorists-bavolek/

Beach schools

https://www.forestschools.com/pages/beach_schools?srsltid=AfmBOopsKCN8eygJE9gFdzUY5W_DQVpi7HIKDgn5RlmRc2lmesNttwlT

Belsky

https://www.child-encyclopedia.com/pdf/expert/child-care-early-childhood-education-and-care/according-experts/child-care-and-its-impact-young

Bourdieu

Irvine, K. (2022). Pierre Bourdieu (1930–2002). In Bradbury, A., and Swailes, R. (eds.), *Early Childhood Theories Today*. London: Learning Matters.

Bowlby

https://www.theeducationpeople.org/blog/exploring-pedagogy-introducing-john-bowlby/

Bronfenbrenner

Grimmer, T. (2022). Urie Bronfenbrenner (1917–2005). In Bradbury, A., and Swailes, R. (eds.), *Early Childhood Theories Today* (pp. 18–31). London: Learning Matters. https://thevoiceofearlychildhood.com/early-childhood-pioneers/urie-bronfenbrenner-2/

Bruner

https://psychology.fas.harvard.edu/people/jerome-bruner

Chomsky

https://www.tutor2u.net/hsc/reference/chomsky-language-acquisition-in-infancy-and-early-childhood

Curiosity approach

https://www.thecuriosityapproach.com/
https://kinderly.co.uk/tag/curiosity-approach/

Dewey

https://www.earlyyears.tv/john-dewey-pioneering-theories-on-early-years-education/#:~:text=Dewey's%20work%20offers%20valuable%20insights,their%20experiences%20promotes%20deeper%20learning.

Dweck

https://www.ted.com/talks/carol_dweck_the_power_of_believing_that_you_can_improve?language=en

Erikson

https://www.earlyyears.tv/erik-erikson-psychosocial-development/#

Forest schools

https://forestschoolassociation.org/
https://www.sirenfilms.co.uk/library/find-out-the-nitty-gritty-of-setting-up-and-running-a-forest-nursery-2/
Videos—https://www.sirenfilms.co.uk/library/the-motivation-for-developing-a-forest-nursery/

Freire

https://www.yorku.ca/cerlac/events/paulo-freire-and-early-childhood-notes-on-the-significance-of-a-non-chronological-childhood-in-education/

Freud

https://thevoiceofearlychildhood.com/early-childhood-pioneers/sigmund-freud-2/

Froebel

https://www.communityplaythings.co.uk/learning-library/articles/what-we-can-learn-from-froebels-kindergarten
https://froebel.org.uk/
https://thefroebelpartnership.co.uk/wp-content/uploads/2024/07/Guildford-Nursery-School-brochure-Feb-2023.pdf
https://guildfordnscc.surrey.sch.uk
Rose, M. (2022). Friedrich Froebel (1782–1852). In Bradbury, A., and Swailes, R. (eds.), *Early Childhood Theories Today*. London: Learning Matters.

FURTHER READING AND RESOURCES

Goldschmidt

https://early-education.org.uk/treasure-baskets-and-heuristic-play/

Gussin-Paley

https://helicopterstories.co.uk/vivian-gussin-paley/

Helicopter stories

https://helicopterstories.co.uk/about-trisha-lee/
https://www.youtube.com/watch?v=38CXtfZULSg

Heuristic play and treasure baskets

https://www.communityplaythings.co.uk/learning-library/articles/heuristic-play?srsltid=AfmBOorOJ0RYwik6EczhqJXXUA7e5fbI0yQyOYGex-g9gDQ4vUQJ3XAR
https://www.youtube.com/watch?v=HfqpZpqAEn0

High/Scope

https://www.communityplaythings.co.uk/learning-library/articles/high-scope
https://highscope.org/
Wiltshire, M. (2018). *Understanding the HighScope Approach: Early Years Education in Practice*. Abingdon: Routledge.

115

Hygge

https://www.nurseryworld.co.uk/content/opinion/feel-the-warm-embrace-of-hygge

Smith, K. (2022). *Bringing Hygge into the Early Years: A Step-by-Step Guide to Bring a Calm and Slow Approach to Your Teaching.* Abingdon: Routledge.

In the moment planning

Ephgrave, A. (2018). *Planning in the Moment with Young Children: A Practical Guide for Early Years Practitioners and Parents.* London: Routledge.

Video—https://www.youtube.com/watch?v=efeizNuuEo0&t=15s

Issacs

https://www.nurseryworld.co.uk/content/features/early-years-pioneers-susan-isaacs

https://thevoiceofearlychildhood.com/early-childhood-pioneers/susan-isaacs-2/

Key person approach

https://kinderly.co.uk/2024/03/14/the-importance-of-the-key-person-approach/

Kohlberg

https://www.simplypsychology.org/kohlberg.html
https://www.youtube.com/watch?v=bounwXLkme4

Laevers

Leuven Scales Booklet—https://emotionallyhealthyschools.org/wp-content/uploads/2020/09/sics-ziko-manual.pdf
https://www.famly.co/blog/leuven-scales-early-years
https://www.nurseryworld.co.uk/content/features/early-years-pioneers-ferre-laevers

Loving pedagogy

Grimmer, T. (2023). Is there a place for love in an early childhood setting? *Early Years: An International Research Journal*, 44(5), 1–44. https://doi.org/10.1080/09575146.2023.2182739
https://www.tamsingrimmer.com/loving-pedagogy

Malaguzzi

https://www.reggiochildren.it/en/reggio-emilia-approach/loris-malaguzzi/
https://thevoiceofearlychildhood.com/early-childhood-pioneers/loris-malaguzzi/

Maslow

https://www.communityplaythings.co.uk/learning-library/articles/living-model?srsltid=AfmBOor-tD-_GEaAq8oqyRIsw2yaxtosPn5r-dBWfzfaTuukFZjmcl2B
https://www.theeducationpeople.org/blog/exploring-pedagogy-introducing-abraham-maslow/

McMillan

https://www.nurseryworld.co.uk/content/features/early-years-pioneers-margaret-and-rachel-mcmillan/

Montessori

Allingham, S. (2022). Maria Montessori (1870–1952). In Bradbury, A., and Swailes, R. (eds.), *Early Childhood Theories Today*. London: Learning Matters.
https://www.youtube.com/watch?v=Ljuw3grZ11Q&pp=ygUVbW9udGVzc29yaSBleHBsYWluZWQg

Parten

https://www.communityplaythings.co.uk/learning-library/articles/mildred-parten-and-her-six-stages-of-play

Pavlov

https://www.firstdiscoverers.co.uk/ivan-pavlov-child-development-theories/

Pedagogy

https://www.tamsingrimmer.com/loving-pedagogy#:~:text=What%20are%20pedagogical,other%20prosocial%20behaviours.

Piaget

https://www.earlyyears.tv/piagets-theory-of-cognitive-development/
https://thevoiceofearlychildhood.com/early-childhood-pioneers/jean-piaget-2/

Pikler approach

https://www.nurseryworld.co.uk/features/article/eyfs-best-practice-all-about-pikler
https://pikler.co.uk/about

Professional love

https://www.pacey.org.uk/news-and-views/pacey-blog/2016/july-2016/'professional-love'-in-early-years-settings/

Reggio Emelia

https://www.youtube.com/watch?v=7n2hCebmT4c&pp=ygUYcmVnZ2lvIGVtaWxpYSBleHBsYWluZWQg

Scaffolding

https://www.youtube.com/watch?v=rVaRdVt6Ihw&pp=ygUXc2NhZmZvbGRpbmcgZWFybHkgeWVhcnM%3D

Schema theory

https://www.communityplaythings.co.uk/learning-library/articles/schemas-by-stella-louis
https://schemaplay.com/

Skinner

https://www.nurseryworld.co.uk/features/article/early-years-pioneers-burrhus-skinner

Slow pedagogy

Clark, A. (2023). *Slow Knowledge and the Unhurried Child: Time for Slow Pedagogies in Early Childhood Education*. Abingdon: Routledge.

https://www.nurseryworld.co.uk/content/features/alison-clarks-slow-pedagogy-how-to-be-slow-outdoors
https://www.youtube.com/watch?v=4HI-Xa9X0AU&pp=ygUNc2xvdyBwZWRhZ29neQ%3D%3D

Steiner

https://www.youtube.com/watch?v=9RbzAY09JWA&pp=ygUSc3Rla W5lciBleHBsYWluZWQg
https://waldorfeducation.uk/

Te Whāriki

Ministry of Education. (2017). *Te Whāriki: He whāriki mātauranga mō ngā mokopuna o Aotearoa Early Childhood Curriculum.* https://www.education.govt.nz/assets/Documents/Early-Childhood/Te-Whariki-Early-Childhood-Curriculum-ENG-Web.pdf
https://www.youtube.com/watch?v=kLkzctGDeEs

Trauma-informed practice

https://www.bristolearlyyears.org.uk/trauma-informed-practice/an-introduction-to-trauma-informed-practice/
https://www.ncb.org.uk/sites/default/files/uploads/attachments/ABS%20Insight%204%20-%20Trauma%20Informed%20Practice%20-%20FINAL%20lo-res.pdf

Treasure baskets

https://www.communityplaythings.co.uk/learning-library/articles/treasure-baskets?srsltid=AfmBOooRfTJOS3sf6fVLOjypJGtcVm-K0SIj1q0CiGnoG3D-Az6y6YvH
https://early-education.org.uk/treasure-baskets-and-heuristic-play/

Vygotsky

https://thevoiceofearlychildhood.com/early-childhood-pioneers/lev-vygotsky/

Waldorf

https://waldorfeducation.uk/

Winnicott

https://www.centreforperinatalpsychology.com.au/good-enough-parent/
https://www.nurseryworld.co.uk/content/features/learning-development-early-years-pioneers-d-w-winnicott

Zone of Proximal Development

https://www.sciencedirect.com/topics/psychology/zone-of-proximal-development
https://www.simplypsychology.org/zone-of-proximal-development.html

References

Part 1

1. Ainsworth, M., and Bell, S. (1970). Attachment, exploration, and separation: Illustrated by the behavior of one-year-olds in a strange situation. *Child Development,* 41(1), 49–67.
2. Duschinsky, R. (2020). Mary Ainsworth and the strange situation procedure. In *Cornerstones of Attachment Research* (online ed.). Oxford: Oxford Academic. https://doi.org/10.1093/med-psych/9780198842064.003.0002, accessed July 21, 2024.
3. Main, M., and Solomon, J. (1986). Discovery of a new, insecure-disorganized/disoriented Attachment Pattern. In Brazelton, T. B., and Yogman M. (eds.), *Affective Development in Infancy.* Ablex.
4. Daniel, V. (2023). *Anti-Racist Practice in the Early Years a Holistic Framework for the Wellbeing of All Children.* Abingdon: Routledge.
5. https://early-education.org.uk/guest-blog-from-rachna-joshi-anti-racism-in-the-early-years/
6. Athey, C. (2007). *Extending Thought in Young Children: A Parent–Teacher Partnership* (p. 50, 2nd ed.). London: Sage.
7. Bowlby, J. (1953). *Childcare and the Growth of Love.* London: Penguin Books.
8. Wilson-Ali, N., Barratt-Pugh, C., and Knaus, M. (2019). Multiple perspectives on attachment theory: Investigating educators' knowledge and understanding. *Australasian Journal of Early Childhood,* 44(3), 215–229.
9. Bandura, A. (1977). *Social Learning Theory.* Englewood Cliffs, NJ: Prentice-Hall.

10. https://www.researchgate.net/profile/Mohammad-Bijandi/publication/367203768_Bandura's_Social_Learning_Theory_Social_Cognitive_Learning_Theory/links/63c6a10bd7e5841e0bd70276/Banduras-Social-Learning-Theory-Social-Cognitive-Learning-Theory.pdf
11. https://www.wgu.edu/blog/guide-social-learning-theory-education2005.html
12. Bradbury, A. (2022). Bavolek. In Bradbury, A., and Swailes, R. (eds.), *Early Childhood Theories Today*. Thousand Oaks, CA: Learning Matters.
13. https://www.earlyyearseducator.co.uk/features/article/beach-schools-the-origins-benefits-and-challenges
14. Belsky, J. (1984). The determinants of parenting: A process model. *Child Development*, 55(1), 83–96.
15. Taraban, L., and Shaw, D. S. (2018). Parenting in context: Revisiting Belsky's classic process of parenting model in early childhood. *Developmental Review*, 48, 55–81.
16. https://www.tutor2u.net/sociology/reference/conflict-theories-of-education-bourdieu-on-cultural-capital
17. Irvine, K. (2022). Pierre Bourdieu (1930–2002). In Bradbury, A., and Swailes, R. (eds.), *Early Childhood Theories Today*. London: Learning Matters.
18. https://www.gov.uk/government/publications/school-inspection-handbook-eif/school-inspection-handbook-for-september-2023
19. Bronfenbrenner, U. (1979). *The Ecology of Human Development: Experiments by Nature and Design*. Boston, MA: Harvard University Press.
20. Crawford, M. (2020). Ecological systems theory: Exploring the development of the theoretical framework as conceived by Bronfenbrenner. *Journal of Public Health Issues and Practices*, 4(2), 170. https://doi.org/10.33790/jphip1100170
21. Grimmer, T. (2022). Chapter 2: Urie Bronfenbrenner. In Bradbury, A., and Swailes, R. (eds.), *Early Childhood Theories Today*. London: Learning Matters.
22. Bruner, J. (1996). *The Culture of Education*. Cambridge, MA: Harvard University Press.
23. Chomsky, N. (1965). *Aspects of the Theory of Syntax*. MIT Press.

REFERENCES

24. Main, P (2023). *Chomsky's Theory.* https://www.structural-learning.com/post/chomskys-theory
25. https://learningjournals.co.uk/what-is-the-curiosity-approach-and-why-is-it-important/#:~:text=Instead%20of%20directing%20children%2C%20and,thinking%2C%20and%20problem%20solving%20skills
26. https://www.thecuriosityapproach.com
27. Dewey, J. (1938). *Logic: The Theory of Inquiry.* Troy, MN: Henry Holt.
28. https://www.earlychildhoodeducationandcare.com/bloggers/2023/3/29/ng8mtx5onwqcvm8i0q6us3jlzz4ukz#:~:text=Dewey%20believed%20that%20children%20learn,and%20experiment%20with%20their%20surroundings
29. Dweck, C. S. (1999). *Self-Theories: Their Role in Motivation, Personality, and Development.* London: Routledge.
30. https://www.parenta.com/2022/02/01/growth-mindset-and-the-theories-of-carol-dweck-part-1/
31. https://www.nurseryworld.co.uk/features/article/a-unique-child-child-development-all-in-the-mindset
32. Erikson, E. (1980). *Identity and the Life Cycle.* New York: W. W. Norton & Company.
33. https://www.earlyyears.tv/erik-erikson-psychosocial-development/#
34. https://forestschoolassociation.org/what-is-forest-school/
35. Jemal A. (2017, November). Critical consciousness: A critique and critical analysis of the literature. *Urban Revivo,* 49(4), 602–626. https://doi.org/10.1007/s11256-017-0411-3.
36. https://www.researchgate.net/profile/David-Lester-3/publication/327477269_Suicide_from_a_psychological_perspective/links/5b9179d092851c78c4f3b5d3/Suicide-from-a-psychological-perspective.pdf#page=9
37. https://iastate.pressbooks.pub/individualfamilydevelopment/chapter/freuds-psychodynamic-theory/
38. https://early-education.org.uk/friedrich-froebel/
39. https://www.froebel.org.uk/about-us/froebelian-principles
40. https://blog.portobelloinstitute.com/vivian-gussin-paleys-methods-of-supporting-language-and-literature-in-early-years
41. https://www.communityplaythings.co.uk/learning-library/articles/heuristic-play

42. https://helicopterstories.co.uk/about-trisha-lee/
43. https://www.communityplaythings.co.uk/learning-library/articles/heuristic-play
44. https://early-education.org.uk/treasure-baskets-and-heuristic-play/
45. https://highscope.org/our-approach/
46. Schweinhart, L. (2005). *The High/Scope Perry Preschool Study Through Age 40: Summary, Conclusions, and Frequently Asked Questions*. High/Scope Educational Research Foundation. https://highscope.org/wp-content/uploads/2018/11/perry-preschool-summary-40.pdf
47. Smith, K. (2022). *Bringing Hygge into the Early Years: A Step-by-Step Guide to Bring a Calm and Slow Approach to Your Teaching*. Abingdon: Routledge.
48. https://www.thecuriosityapproach.com/blog/hygge-in-the-early-years#:~:text=Hygge%20(pronounced%20hue%2Dguh%20not,%2Dbeing%2C%20togetherness%20and%20friendship
49. Ephgrave, A. (2018). *Planning in the Moment with Young Children: A Practical Guide for Early Years Practitioners and Parents*. London: Routledge.
50. https://learningjournals.co.uk/benefits-of-using-in-the-moment-planning-for-young-children/
51. https://eyfs.info/articles.html/teaching-and-learning/educational-pioneers-susan-isaacs-1885-1948-r40/
52. https://thevoiceofearlychildhood.com/early-childhood-pioneers/susan-isaacs-2/
53. https://birthto5matters.org.uk/attachment-and-the-role-of-the-key-person/
54. https://www.verywellmind.com/kohlbergs-theory-of-moral-development-2795071#:~:text=Kohlberg's%20theory%20suggests%20that%20moral,as%20part%20of%20this%20process
55. Kohlberg, L. (1966). A cognitive-developmental analysis of children's sex-role concepts and attitudes. In Maecoby, E. E. (ed.), *The Development of Sex Differences*. Stanford, CA: Stanford University Press.
56. Laevers, F. (2005). *Well-Being and Involvement in Care Settings. A Process-Oriented Self-Evaluation Instrument*. Leuven: Kind & Gezin and Research Centre for Experiential Education.

REFERENCES

57. Grimmer, T. (2021). *Developing a Loving Pedagogy in the Early Years: How Love Fits with Professional Practice*. Abingdon: Routledge.
58. Edwards, C., Gandini, L., and Forman, G. (2012). *The Hundred Languages of Children: The Reggio Emilia Experience in Transformation* (3rd ed.). Santa Barbara, CA: Praeger.
59. Maslow, A. (1943). A theory of human motivation. *Psychological Review*, 50(4), 370–396.
60. Clough, P., and Nutbrown, C. (2016). Rachel and margaret McMillian: Practice and politics. In David, T., Goouch, K., and Powell, S. (eds.), *The Routledge International Handbook of Philosophies and Theories of Early Childhood Education and Care*. Abingdon: Routledge.
61. https://childcarestudies.co.uk/2021/07/09/margaret-mcmillan/
62. Montessori, M. (1912). *The Montessori Method* (Translated by A. E. George). New York: Fredrick. A Stokes Company.
63. Parten, M. B. (1933). Social play among preschool children. *The Journal of Abnormal and Social Psychology*, 28(2), 136–147.
64. https://www.communityplaythings.co.uk/learning-library/articles/mildred-parten-and-her-six-stages-of-play
65. https://brightestbeginning.com/stages-of-play/
66. https://www.firstdiscoverers.co.uk/ivan-pavlov-child-development-theories/
67. https://courses.lumenlearning.com/suny-fmcc-childhood-psychology/chapter/how-do-we-act-exploring-behavior/
68. https://www.tamsingrimmer.com/loving-pedagogy
69. Piaget, J. (1971). The theory of stages in cognitive development. In Green, D. R., Ford, M. P., and Flamer, G. B. (eds.), *Measurement and Piaget*. McGraw-Hill.
70. https://www.earlyyears.tv/piagets-theory-of-cognitive-development/
71. https://pikler.co.uk/
72. https://cris.brighton.ac.uk/ws/portalfiles/portal/490126/Characterising%20the%20Principles%20of%20Professional%20Love%20accepted%20version%20for%20publication%20(%20author's%20final%20version).pdf
73. https://static1.squarespace.com/static/51ed94d0e4b03bd18bdcc998/t/526c8eabe4b0f35a9f0216e3/1382846123076/ExaminingtheReggioEmiliaApproach.pdf

74. https://www.pacey.org.uk/Pacey/media/Website-files/PACEY%20member%20practice%20guides%20(PDFs)/PG28-Theories-of-child-development.pdf
75. Grimmer, T. (2017). *Observing and Developing Schematic Behaviour in Young Children: A Professional's Guide for Supporting Children's Learning, Play and Development.* London: Jessica Kingsley Publishers.
76. https://www.communityplaythings.co.uk/learning-library/articles/schemas-by-stella-louis
77. https://www.firstdiscoverers.co.uk/b-f-skinner-child-development-theories/
78. Clark, A. (2023). *Slow Knowledge and the Unhurried Child: Time for Slow Pedagogies in Early Childhood Education.* Abingdon: Routledge.
79. https://waldorfeducation.uk/
80. https://www.nurseryworld.co.uk/features/article/eyfs-best-practice-all-about-steiner-waldorf-education
81. https://www.waldorfeducation.org/waldorf-education/rudolf-steiner-the-history-of-waldorf-education
82. Ministry of Education. (2017). *Te Whāriki: He whāriki mātauranga mō ngā mokopuna o Aotearoa Early Childhood Curriculum.* https://www.education.govt.nz/assets/Documents/Early-Childhood/Te-Whariki-Early-Childhood-Curriculum-ENG-Web.pdf
83. https://www.famly.co/blog/te-whariki-new-zealand-early-years-curriculum
84. https://www.bristolearlyyears.org.uk/trauma-informed-practice/an-introduction-to-trauma-informed-practice/
85. Nicholson, J., Perez, P., Kurtz, J., and Bryant, S. (2023). *Trauma-Informed Practices for Early Childhood Educators: Relationship-Based Approaches That Reduce Stress, Build Resilience and Support Healing in Young Children.* New York: Routledge.
86. https://www.teachearlyyears.com/learning-and-development/view/making-treasure-baskets
87. Vygotsky, L. S. (1978). *Mind in Society: The Development of Higher Mental Processes.* Cambridge, MA: Harvard University Press.
88. https://www.theeducationpeople.org/blog/exploring-pedagogy-introducing-lev-vygotsky/#:~:text=Lev%20Vygotsky%20was%20born%20in,school%20achieving%20a%20formal%20degree

89. Winnicott, D. W. (1971). *Playing and Reality.* Penguin.
90. https://www.wested.org/resources/zone-of-proximal-development/#:~:text=The%20Zone%20of%20Proximal%20Development,collaboration%20with%20more%20capable%20peers

Part 2
Applying these theories to practice

Part 1 of this book provided an overview of the different theories, theorists, and approaches to early childhood education. It included examples of settings and of how early years professionals and practitioners have put these theories into practice, recording their experiences, findings, and beliefs as a result of seeing these theories applied.

In this section of the book, we will look more broadly at the ethos of the setting/school and how early childhood settings can embed these theories and approaches into everyday practice.

The areas this section will explore are:

- The importance of embedding theories/approaches that encapsulate the beliefs of the setting as a community
- How settings can begin to incorporate and follow new beliefs/ideas/approaches
- Staff training
- Parental involvement
- Challenges of embedding new theories and approaches
- Benefits of adopting/embedding new theories and approaches to early childhood education
- Behavioural implications of adopting new theories and approaches
- How to write a policy on pedagogy
- Questions for reflection

DOI: 10.4324/9781032691367-59

The importance of embedding theories/approaches that encapsulate the beliefs of the setting as a community

Early years education and our understanding of child development and neuroscience are ever-changing. As practitioners, it is essential that we are aware of, investigate, and stay up to date with research and information so that we are prepared to reflect on, adapt, and adopt this new information to best support the children we care for.

Each setting will have its own belief system, pedagogy, and ethos, and it is essential that every single person working with children within the setting has the same beliefs about the pedagogy and ethos so that there is cohesion and consistency in the teaching and environment that children experience during their time at the setting.

If new theories/approaches come to light as a result of extensive research and a senior member of the team decides that, as a setting, they should adopt these new theories and approaches to education, they must first ensure that the theories and approaches they propose to follow are consistent not only with the belief system of the setting as a whole community but of the individual practitioners working within the setting.

Children learn best when they are taught and supported by loving, knowledgeable practitioners who truly believe and have faith in the curriculum and ethos they follow. So if the community does not support/believe in the theories and approaches a setting wishes to adopt, this will have a detrimental impact on the quality of teaching and learning within the setting, potentially hindering children's development.

How settings can begin to incorporate and follow new beliefs/ ideas/approaches

A starting point for incorporating new beliefs, ideas, and approaches into the setting should always be an open discussion with all staff members to share the findings of the research, discuss how these theories and approaches would fit with the culture of the setting as it stands, and weigh up the benefits of adopting these new approaches and embedding them in the ethos and curriculum of the setting.

Managers/owners putting forward these new ideas and approaches should come equipped with research, findings, and case studies and be prepared to answer any questions staff may have. Similarly, leaders should come armed with a plan/overview of how adopting these approaches will look and work in practice and outline clearly how that will look for both staff and children.

Staff training

Training of staff is a key component for any setting but even more so when adopting and embedding new theories and beliefs. Leaders should endeavour to ensure that the training they provide for staff, whether it be external or internal, is high quality, informative, and engaging and suits the individual staff members' learning styles. Training is just like teaching: there is no "one size fits all" approach for adults. Learners need variety and flexibility, and what works for one might not work for another. So finding training that suits a variety of learning styles is imperative, particularly when it requires staff to adopt new belief systems alongside potentially learning new skills and teaching methods.

Staff should also have opportunities to practice new skills and put into practice the things they've learned on numerous occasions before being expected to teach and embed these new skills in their everyday practice. This is where peer observation and review systems come into play, as they are very efficient learning tools.

A number of different consultants and organisations offer training and Continuing Professional Development about early childhood theories and approaches. I suggest looking up organisations such as Early Education and Early Excellence. In addition, Kathy Brodie regularly has speakers on Early Years TV covering subjects that link with approaches and pedagogies. A number of platforms such as Kinderly, Parenta, and Famly offer training, advice, and support in this area.[1-6]

Parental involvement

As we know, in early education, parental involvement and engagement are key in supporting children's learning and development. Parents are a child's primary educators, and it is essential that their input, views, and knowledge be respected and welcomed.

It is also essential that when we are looking to embed new approaches into the curriculum, we consult and discuss with all parents of children in the setting prior to implementing any of our findings/ideas. Parents and families make up the community of a setting, so it is imperative that they be involved in the decision-making process of embedding new beliefs and ideas in its curriculum and ethos.

We can work to engage with parents via a number of ways, such as:

- Newsletters
- Social media updates
- Open days
- Informal chats
- Information evenings
- Emails
- Posters around the setting
- Phone calls
- Updates on the child's learning platform

Challenges of embedding new theories and approaches

Change is difficult for everyone, so big changes or new approaches to teaching and learning should be approached sensitively, with everyone's viewpoints and concerns respected and valued. Some staff may take more time to accept the idea of such a significant change and may need more support or training before they feel comfortable enough to put new approaches into practice.

Similarly, some parents/families may not be receptive to the idea of significant change to the ethos of the setting and may not be supportive until they see the benefits and positive impact for themselves. It is essential that we respect these differences and do all we can to support families and allow ample opportunities for parents and carers to come in, spend time in the setting, and see the changes in action for themselves, regardless of how long this may take.

Benefits of adopting/embedding new theories and approaches to early childhood education

Research-based practice and new ideas and information have endless benefits for settings, teaching, learning, and children that far outweigh the challenges and difficulties we may encounter by adopting and embedding new routines and practices.[7]

Learning environments can become more engaging, exciting, and interactive, helping children feel empowered and respected. Practitioners ignite their passion and deepen their beliefs, which not only is wonderful for them professionally and personally but also enhances the quality of their teaching. This, in turn, has endless benefits and positive impact on the children in their care via holistic learning and development.

Similarly, when a staff team works collaboratively towards a shared goal with endless positive outcomes, the culture and morale of the setting are positively impacted, too, reducing workplace stress and supporting practitioner well-being.

Behavioural implications of adopting new theories and approaches

Children find change especially difficult, and transitions may have implications for their learning and development. Their behaviour may change during this period, too, and we must be prepared and sympathetic to this. For some children, even the most subtle of changes can be unsettling. So just as we consult and discuss with staff and parents, where it is developmentally appropriate, we must ensure that children are aware, to some degree, of the changes that will be taking place, however trivial they might seem to us as adults.

This links with the United Nations Convention on the Rights of the Child, specifically Article 12, which says children should have a say in matters that affect them. By sharing changes with children and consulting with them, we are putting this right into action.

Adopting new beliefs and changing the way in which we teach and learn can alter the parameters for children. This can result in them behaving in uncharacteristic ways. When supporting staff in implementing changes, we must ensure all staff are sensitive to how change can impact the children, too, and work collectively to minimise the impact on the children's learning, development, emotions, and behaviours.

Ways that we can minimise the impact of any change on our children include:

- Creating a sense of belonging and collective ownership within our setting
- Talking to children about our provision regularly

DOI: 10.4324/9781032691367-66

- Asking or ascertaining children's views about our provision
- Explaining changes in developmentally appropriate language
- Reassuring the children about what will stay the same as well as highlighting differences
- Liaising fully with parents and families about changes
- Creating as much consistency as possible within the setting
- Ensuring all staff understand the impact on the children and respond sensitively

How to write a policy on pedagogy

A clearly written policy is a crucial document for any early years setting. There should be a policy outlining the educational philosophy and teaching practices that will guide the development and learning of young children in the setting during their time there.

If a setting adopts a new pedagogy or incorporates different philosophies into the setting, this policy should be reviewed, amended, and shared with staff and parents.

A well-crafted policy ensures consistency, quality, and a shared understanding among practitioners, parents, and stakeholders.

Key elements of an early years pedagogy policy

1. **Vision and values**
   - **Statement of intent:** Begin with a clear statement of the setting's educational philosophy. This should reflect a commitment to high-quality early childhood education.
   - **Core values:** Outline the core values that underpin your approach, such as respect, inclusivity, and a commitment to fostering a love of learning.
2. **Legal and regulatory framework**
   - **EYFS compliance:** Ensure your policy aligns with the Early Years Foundation Stage framework, which sets the standards for the learning, development, and care of children from birth to 5 years old.
   - **Safeguarding:** Incorporate safeguarding principles to ensure the safety and well-being of children.

3. **Pedagogical approaches**
   - **Child-centred learning:** Emphasise the importance of placing the child at the centre of the learning process. This includes recognising each child's unique needs, interests, and developmental stage.
   - **Play-based learning:** Highlight the role of play in early years education. Play is a primary way through which children learn and develop.
   - **Observations and assessments:** Discuss the methods for observing and assessing children's progress to inform planning and support individual learning paths.
4. **Learning environment**
   - **Inclusive environment:** Describe how the learning environment will be inclusive, welcoming, and accessible to all children.
   - **Indoor and outdoor learning:** Detail the importance of both indoor and outdoor learning experiences. Outdoor play is vital for physical development and connecting with nature.
5. **Curriculum and planning**
   - **Holistic development:** Ensure the curriculum supports all areas of a child's development, including physical, emotional, social, and cognitive.
   - **Flexible planning:** Outline how planning will be flexible to respond to children's emerging interests and needs.
6. **Partnership with parents and community**
   - **Parent engagement:** Explain how the setting will engage with parents and carers, recognising them as partners in their children's education.
   - **Community links:** Describe how the setting will build links with the local community to enhance children's learning experiences.
7. **Continuous professional development**
   - **Staff training:** Emphasise the importance of ongoing professional development for staff to stay updated with best practices in early years education.
   - **Reflective practice:** Encourage reflective practice among practitioners to continuously improve their teaching strategies and outcomes for children.

Creating an early years policy is a collaborative and evolving process. By clearly articulating your educational philosophy and practices, you ensure that all children in your setting receive the highest quality of care and education and that every person who is part of the community of your setting knows, understands, and shares the same values and beliefs and knows how they look in practice.

Remember, the policy should be a living document that grows and adapts with your setting and the children you care for. Any changes or new approaches should be reviewed and incorporated into the policy.

Questions for reflection

I thought it fitting that I end this book with some questions through which you might reflect upon your own provision. If you work with others, answer them honestly as a team; the perspective of all team members is valid and valuable. To gain a holistic view, you may want to include the voice of the child(ren), practitioners, parents, leadership team, and other stakeholders.

- What does your ethos say about your setting and your views of children and childhood?
- What pedagogies and principles underpin your practice?
- Does your day-to-day practice typically reflect your ethos?
- How do you articulate your values and pedagogy to others?
- Do you have a policy about pedagogy which is regularly reviewed and understood by everyone?
- Is your pedagogical approach outlined in any public materials, e.g. website, prospectus, advertisements?
- To what extent do you take the views of children, parents, and staff into consideration when making decisions?
- How do you ensure that all staff are up to date in their knowledge, training, and skills?
- How well does your provision meet the individual needs of the children who attend?
- Consider how the setting feels from different perspectives. What is it like to be in leadership in this setting? Or a cleaner? Or a parent-helper? Or a governor? Is it welcoming, loving, and inclusive?
- How could you celebrate your pedagogy and principles with others?

Conclusion

This book has shared and explained a variety of theories and approaches within early childhood development education. I hope that it has been helpful as you reflect upon your own philosophy and approach in your setting.

Adopting and implementing new research, theories, and approaches is a daunting process, but it is beneficial to children's learning and development. If your setting discovers a new approach to early childhood education and truly believes it provides an opportunity to enrich the learning and development of the children in your care, implementing new skills, ideas, and learning experiences and embedding these them in the ethos of your setting will provide the most incredible benefits and learning opportunities for not only the children in your care but your staff team too.

References

Part 2

1. Early Education—https://early-education.org.uk/
2. Early Excellence—https://training.earlyexcellence.com/w/uk/
3. Early Years TV—https://www.earlyyears.tv/
4. Kinderly—https://kinderly.co.uk/news-and-media/
5. Parenta—https://www.parenta.com/
6. Famly—https://www.famly.co/
7. UNICEF. (1989). *United Nations Convention on the Rights of the Child.* www.unicef.org.uk/Documents/Publication-pdfs/UNCRC_PRESS200910web.pdf

Index

accommodation 10
Ainsworth, Mary 7, 13, 110
ako concept 100
Albion, Jo 97
anal stage 41
anti-racist practice 8–9, 110
anxious-ambivalent attachment 13
anxious-avoidant attachment 13
assimilation 10
associative play 80
Athey, Chris 10–11, 110
attachment-aware environments 102–103
attachment styles 7, 13, 102
attachment theory 13; Ainsworth and 7, 13, 110; Bowlby and 13, 23; resources 111
autonomy 96

Bandura, Albert 14–15, 111
Bartlett, Frederic 93
Bavolek, Stephen 16–17, 111
beach schools 18–20, 111
Belsky, Jay 21, 112
Bennett, Stephanie 30
biases 8–9
Bobo doll experiments 14
Bourdieu, Pierre 22, 112
Bowlby, John 7, 13, 23, 112
Bronfenbrenner, Urie 24–25, 112
Bruce, Tina 43
Bruner, Jerome 26–27, 93, 112

case studies: beach schools—a nanny perspective 18–20; forest schools 37–38; Guildford Nursery School 43–45; helicopter stories 49–51; imitation/role-modelling—a nanny perspective 15; In-The-Moment Planning (ITMP) 60–62; language development 28–29; Leuven scales 70; Loving Pedagogy 71–72; *see also* childminder's perspective
Cave, Sally 43–45
child development, Piaget's theory of 41, 84–85
child-led learning 63–64; Curiosity Approach and 30; In-The-Moment Planning (ITMP) 60; Isaacs's approach and 63–64; Montessori approach and 77
childminder's perspective: attachment to transitional objects 106–107; Hygge approach and 57–58; Reggio Emilia and 91–92; theory of psychosocial development 35–36
Chomsky, Noam 28, 113
chronosystem 24
Cinnamon Brow School Pre-School Nursery 49–51
Clark, Alison 97
classical conditioning 81–82

147

INDEX

cognitive development: Bruner and 27; McMillan sisters and 75; Page and 88; Piaget and 84–85; Piaget's stages of 84–85; schema theory and 93–94; Te Whāriki and 100; Vygotsky and 105
cognitive growth 52
community support systems 17
concentric circles 24
concrete learning materials 78
concrete operational stage of cognitive development 84–85
confidence: Bavolek's theory and 16; beach schools and 19; Bowlby's theory and 23; Curiosity Approach and 30; Helicopter Stories approach and 49, 50, 51; heuristic play and treasure baskets and 53
Conkbayir, Mine 35–36
continuous reinforcement 96
conventional level of moral development 66
cooperative play 80
coping skills, resilience and 17
cosiness *see* Hygge
creativity: Athey's approach and 11; Chomsky's approach and 28; Cultural Capital and 22; Curiosity Approach and 30; forest schools and 37; Froebel's approach and 42, 43; Helicopter Stories approach and 49; heuristic play and treasure baskets and 52, 53; Malaguzzi's approach and 73; Reggio Emilia approach and 90; Steiner's approach and 98, 99; Te Whāriki and 101
critical consciousness 39, 40
critical thinking: anti-racist practice and 9; Athey's approach and 11; Chomsky's approach and 28; Curiosity Approach and 30; Freire's approach and 39; heuristic play and treasure baskets and 52; Hygge approach and 57; Isaacs's approach and 63; Steiner's approach and 98
Cultural Capital 22

cultural diversity 100–101
Curiosity Approach 30, 113
curriculum, incorporating multicultural perspectives into 8

Dewey, John 31, 113
dialogue 39, 40, 67
disorganised attachment 7
documentation, in Reggio Emilia approach 91
Dweck, Carol 32–33, 113

early childhood development, Laevers's theory of 69–70
early childhood education: Froebel's theory of 42–45; Vygotsky's theory of 105
early childhood theories and approaches: applying to practice 131; behavioural implications of adopting new 139–140; child development, Piaget's 41, 84–85; classical conditioning 81–82; early childhood development, Laevers's 69–70; early childhood education, Froebel's 42–45; early childhood education, Vygotsky's 105; embedding 133, 137–138; gender constancy 67–68 (*see also* gender development); human development 34; innate language acquisition 28; moral development 66–68; operant conditioning 95, 96; parental involvement 136; psychosocial development 34; questions for reflection 144; rationale for 2; social play 79–80; staff training 135; terms relating to 5–6
ecological model, Belsky's 21
ecological systems theory 24–25
educational model, Steiner's 98–99
education by development 42
embedding theories and approaches: benefits of 138; challenges of 137; importance of 133
emotional warmth and security 88

148

emotion coaching 96
empathy: anti-racist practice and 8; Bavolek's theory and 16; Gussin-Paley's approach and 46; Helicopter Stories and 48, 49, 50–51; Isaacs's and 63, 64; Kohlberg's theory and 66; Montessori approach and 78; Page's Professional Love approach and 88; Steiner's method and 99; trauma-informed or trauma-responsive practice and 102; understanding and 16, 42, 66
enactive mode 27
enclosure schema 94
Erikson, Erik 34, 41, 113
esteem, in hierarchy of needs 74
ethical behaviour 67
ethical considerations 88–89
exosystem 24
exploration: Ainsworth's approach and 13; Athey's approach and 11; Curiosity Approach and 30; forest schools and 37; heuristic play and treasure baskets and 53; high/scope approach and 55; In-The-Moment Planning (ITMP) and 60; Isaacs's approach and 63; Malaguzzi's approach and 73; Montessori approach and 77, 78; Pikler approach and 87; Reggio Emilia approach and 90, 91–92; schema theory and 94; Steiner's approach and 98; Vygotsky's theory and 105

fine motor skills 52
fixed mindset 32
forest schools 37–38, 114
formal operational stage of cognitive development 85
freedom of movement 86
freedom within limits 78
Freire, Paulo 39–40, 114
Freud, Sigmund 41, 114
Froebel, Friedrich 42–45, 114
Froebel Partnership 45

Gare-mogg, Nicky 35–36
gender constancy, theory of 67–68; see also gender development
gender development 67–68; gender constancy 68; gender identity/labelling 67; gender stability 67–68
genital stage 41
Goldschmidt, Elinor 47, 104, 115
good-enough mother 106
gradual fading 27
Grimmer, Tamsin 71–72, 117
growth mindset 32–33
Guildford Nursery School 43–45
Gussin-Paley, Vivian 46, 48, 50, 115

hands-on experiences and learning: assimilation and 10; beach schools and 18; Dewey's approach and 31; Froebel's approach and 42; High/Scope approach and 54; Montessori approach and 77, 78; Steiner's approach and 98–99
Helicopter Stories 46, 115
Hellyn, Lyndsey 30
heuristic play and treasure baskets 47, 52–53, 104, 115
hierarchy of needs 74
high/scope approach 54–55, 115
holistic approach to learning: forest schools and 37; Froebel's 42–43; McMillan sisters' 76; Steiner's 98, 99; Te Whāriki and 100
holistic development 88
human development, theory of 34
Hygge approach 56–58, 116

iconic mode 27
identity development 8
imagination: Helicopter Stories approach and 48, 49; heuristic play and treasure baskets and 52, 53; Steiner's approach and 98, 99; Te Whāriki and 101
imitation 14, 15
implicit bias 8–9

149

inclusive learning environment, creating 8
independence 96; beach schools and 19; Bruner's approach and 27; Curiosity Approach and 30; heuristic play and treasure baskets and 53; Isaacs's approach and 63; Montessori approach and 77; Skinner's theory and 96; Winnicott's approach and 106
inequality: Cultural Capital and 22; Freire's pedagogy and 39, 40
innate language acquisition, theory of 28
insecure-avoidant attachment 7
insecure-resistant attachment 7
intermittent reinforcement 96
In-The-Moment Planning (ITMP) 59–62, 116
intrinsic reinforcement 14–15
Issacs, Susan 63–64, 116

Jack and Jill Community Preschool 71–72

key person approach 13, 65, 116
kindergarten: Froebel's founding of 42; Perry Preschool Study and 54; Waldorf 98
Kohlberg, Laurence 66–68, 117

Laevers, Ferre 69–70, 117
language development: Chomsky's approach and 29; Erikson's theory and 35; heuristic play and treasure baskets and 53
language-rich experiences 35–36
latency stage 41
Lee, Tricia 48
Leuven scales 70, 117
linguistic research 28–29
love and belonging, in hierarchy of needs 74
Loving Pedagogy 71–72, 117
Luckhurst, Elizabeth 38

macrosystem 24
Main, M. 7
Malaguzzi, Loris 73, 90, 117; see also Reggio Emilia
Maslow, Abraham 74, 118
McMillan, Margaret and Rachel 75–76, 118
mesosystem 24
microsystem 24
mindset 32–33
mixed-age groupings 77–78
modelling 14–15, 26, 67
modes of mental representation 27
Montessori 30, 77–78, 118
Montessori, Maria 77
moral development 66–68, 98; Kohlberg's theory and 66–68; Steiner's approach and 98
moral development, theory of 66–68

nature-based education: beach schools's approach to 18; forest schools's approach to 37; McMillan sisters's approach to 75, 76
negative reinforcement 95
nested systems 24
nurturing relationships 16, 65

observational learning: Bandura's theory and 14; beach schools and 18; Gussin-Paley's approach and 46; In-The-Moment Planning (ITMP) and 59, 60, 61, 62; Isaacs's approach and 64; Laevers's approach and 69, 70; Pikler approach and 86; Reggio Emilia approach and 90, 91; schema theory and 94; Strange Situation and 7
onlooker play 79
operant conditioning, Skinner's theory of 95, 96
oral stage 41

Page, Jools 88–89
parallel play 79
parental involvement 136
Parten, Mildred 79–80, 118

INDEX

Pavlov, Ivan 81–82, 119
pedagogy 83, 119; policy on, how to write 141–143
Perry Preschool Study 54
phallic stage 41
physiological needs, in hierarchy of needs 74
Piaget, Jean 41, 84–85, 119
Pikler, Emmi 84–85, 119
Pikler approach 119
plan-do-review process 54
play: Froebel's approach and 42–45; Gussin-Paley's approach and 46; heuristic 47, 104, 115; Isaacs's approach and 63–64; McMillan sisters's approach and 75–76; Parten's stages of 79–80; Te Whāriki approach and 101
positive discipline 16
positive reinforcement 95; Kohlberg's theory and 67; Skinner's theory and 95; trauma-informed or trauma-responsive practice and 102
post-conventional level of moral development 66
pragmatism 31
pre-conventional level of moral development 66
preoperational stage of cognitive development 84
problem-solving abilities: Bavolek's theory and 16; Bruner's theory and 27; Curiosity Approach and 30; Dewey's approach and 31; forest schools and 37; heuristic play and 52; high/scope approach and 54; Hygge approach and 57; McMillan sisters' approach and 75; Piaget's theory and 85; Pikler approach and 87; Te Whāriki and 101
professional boundaries 88
Professional Love 88–89, 119
psychosexual stages 41
psychosocial development, theory of 34–36
punishment 95

reciprocal determinism 15
reflection, questions for 144
Reggio Emelia 30, 73, 90–92, 120
reinforcement schedules 96
relational practice 102
repetition 10–11, 82, 93
resilience: attachment theory 7, 23; building, concept of 16–17, 23; coping skills and 17; forest schools and 37; growth mindset and 32; Professional Love and 89
rhythms and rituals, respect for 87
risk-taking 37
role modelling 14–15, 96
rotation schema 94

safety, in hierarchy of needs 74
scaffolding: Bruner's approach to 26–27; learning stories and 29; operant conditioning and 96; Pikler approach to 86–87; resources 120; schema theory and 93–94; zone of proximal development (ZPD) and 26, 105, 108
schema: definition of 10; in practice 11–12; schematic play 10–12; types of 93–94
schema theory 93–94, 120; assimilation, accommodation and 10–12; benefits of 94; definition and purpose of 93; introduction of 93
schematic play 10–12
secure attachment 7, 13, 23, 102, 106
self-actualisation, in hierarchy of needs 74
self-esteem 8
self-regulation 96
Self-Theories: Their Role in Motivation, Personality, and Development (Dweck) 32
sensitive guidance 26
sensorimotor stage of cognitive development 84
sensory development 52
setbacks 32–33

151

INDEX

settings: as a community, embedding theories/approaches that encapsulate the beliefs of 133; to incorporate and follow new beliefs/ideas/approaches 134
shaping, Skinner's concept of 96
Skinner, B. F. 95–96, 120
slow pedagogy 97, 120–121
social cognitive theory 14
social justice 39, 40
social learning theory 14–15
social play, Parten's stages of 79–80
socio-economic theory 22
socio-emotional development 16, 17
solitary (independent) play 79
Solomon, J. 7
spiral curriculum 27
staff training 135
Steiner, Rudolf 30, 98–99, 121
stereotypes 8, 9
storytelling: acting out stories and 48; Gussin-Paley's approach and 46; Helicopter Stories and 48–51; Kohlberg's theory and 66; reflection and feedback and 48; Steiner's approach and 98
"Strange Situation" procedure 7, 13
structuring tasks 26
symbolic mode 27
systematic racism 8

terms relating to early childhood theories and approaches 5–6
Te Whāriki 30, 100–101, 121
theories *see* early childhood theories and approaches
three-stage system 27

trajectory schema 93
transitional objects 106–107
transporting schema 94
trauma-informed or trauma-responsive practice 102–103, 121
treasure baskets 47, 104, 115, 122
trust in the child 86

understanding, empathy and 16, 42, 66
universal grammar 28
unoccupied play 79

vicarious learning 14
Vygotsky, Lev 93, 105, 108, 122

Waldorf education 98–99, 122
Weikart, David 54
well-being: attachment theory and 7, 16, 23; Bavolek's theories and 16, 17; Erikson's theory of human development and 34; Hygge approach and 56, 57; Isaacs's approach and 63–64; key person approach and 13, 65; Laevers's theory and 69; Loving Pedagogy and 71–72; McMillan sisters' approach and 75, 76; pedagogy policy and 141; Pikler approach and 86, 87; of practitioner 138; Professional Love approach and 89; Te Whāriki and 100; trauma-informed or trauma-responsive practice and 103
Williams-Siegfredsen, Jane 18
Winnicott, Donald 106, 122

Zone of Proximal Development (ZPD) 26, 105, 108, 122

For Product Safety Concerns and Information please contact our EU representative GPSR@taylorandfrancis.com
Taylor & Francis Verlag GmbH, Kaufingerstraße 24, 80331 München, Germany

www.ingramcontent.com/pod-product-compliance
Lightning Source LLC
Chambersburg PA
CBHW050527170426
43201CB00013B/2116